REMNANTS
(A FABLE)

Remnants

(A Fable)

Jason Sherman

Playwrights Canada Press
Toronto • Canada

Playwrights Canada Press

215 Spadina Avenue, Suite 230, Toronto, Ontario CANADA M5T 2C7
416-703-0013
orders@playwrightscanada.com • www.playwrightscanada.com

Playwrights Canada Press acknowledges the support of
the taxpayers of Canada and the province of Ontario through
The Canada Council for the Arts and the Ontario Arts Council.

Cover photo of: (*l to r*) Alex Poch-Goldin, Jerry Franken, Jason Jazrawy,
Victor Ertmanis, Alon Nashman, Dmitry Chepovetsky, Kyle Horton.
Cover photo by Cylla von Tiedemann.
Sketch on inside half-title page by Charlotte Dean.
Book Production/Cover: JLArt

National Library of Canada Cataloguing in Publication

Sherman, Jason, 1962-
    Remnants : a fable / Jason Sherman.

A play.
ISBN 0-88754-716-8

    1. Joseph (Son of Jacob)–Drama. I. Title.

PS8587.H3858R44 2004   C812'.54   C2004-900376-3

First edition: July 2004.
Printed and bound by Hignell Printing at Winnipeg, Canada.

For my mother, Grace Sherman (1927-2004).

—•— Table of Contents —•—

Jason Sherman's plays include *Three in the Back, Two in the Head* (first produced by Tarragon Theatre/Necessary Angel/National Arts Centre), *The Retreat* (Tarragon); *Patience* (Tarragon); *It's All True* (Tarragon); *An Acre of Time* (Great Canadian Theatre Company); *The League of Nathans* (Orange Dog Theatre/Theatre Passe Muraille); *Reading Hebron* (Factory Theatre); and *None is Too Many* (Winnipeg Jewish Theatre/Manitoba Theatre Centre). He has received the Governor General's Award for Drama (and been nominated three other times), and the Chalmers Canadian Play Award (twice, along with three other nominations). He lives in Toronto.

Remnants (A Fable) premiered at Tarragon Theatre, Toronto, September 2003, with the following company:

JUDAH and others	Alex Poch-Goldin
REUBEN and others	Alon Nashman
JOSEPH	Dmitry Chepovetsky
PISCHUK, MACKENZIE KING and others	Victor Ertmanis
JACOB, POTTINGER, BLAIR and others	Jerry Franken
SIMON and others	Jason Jazrawy
BENJAMIN and others	Kyle Horton

Directed by Richard Rose
Assistant Director: Lee Wilson
Set and Lighting designed by Graeme Thomson
Costumes designed by Charlotte Dean
Sound designed by Todd Charlton
Stage Manager: Kathryn Westoll
Apprentice Stage Manager: Michelene A. Sutherland
Script Manager/Researcher: Stephen Colella

— • —

The play was commissioned by the Canadian Stage Company; thanks to Katherine Kaszas, Iris Turcott, Bonnie Green and the following actors who participated in this early stage of the play's development: Michael Ball, Richard Binsley, Shauna Black, John Dolan, Victor Ertmanis, Catherine Hayos, Peter Hutt, Alon Nashman, Jordan Pettle, Rick Roberts, Paul Soles. Stage manager: Janet Gregor.

And very special thanks to the following people for their thoughts, advice and assistance: Norm Bornstein; Stephen Colella; Cheryl Landy; Melinda Little; Ellen Scheinberg (Director of the Ontario Jewish Archives).

2 / Jason Sherman

—•— Characters —•—

JACOB, a tailor – JUDAH, REUBEN, JOSEPH, SIMON, BENJAMIN, his sons – PISCHUK, a servant – IMMIGRATION INSPECTOR – IMMIGRATION OFFICER – PERSONS IN LINE – MAX, an immigrant – CONDUCTOR – CRYING MAN – POTTINGER, factory owner – NIGHT WATCHMAN – BROWN SHIRTS – A SOLDIER – RELIEF WORKER – LAY and MEASURES, former servants to Mackenzie King – FRANCIS BROWN, relief worker – MACKENZIE KING, the Prime Minister – JACK, a servant to King – FREDERIC BLAIR, head of the Immigration Branch – A GUARD.

—•— Sources —•—

Remnants (A Fable) owes its story to the Bible, and many of its contemporary details to the following sources:

• *There Once Was a World: A 900-Year Chronicle of the Shtetl of Eishyshok*, by Yaffa Eliach

• *None is Too Many: Canada and the Jews of Europe 1933-1948*, by Irving Abella and Harold Troper, which also served as the basis for a play I was commissioned to write for the Winnipeg Jewish Theatre (and produced by them, with the Manitoba Theatre Centre, in 1997)

• *The Diaries of William Lyon Mackenzie King*, 1893-1950, a remarkable document, all the more remarkable for being available online—and searchable—at the National Archives of Canada web site http://king.archives.ca/EN/default.asp

• *The Great Depression, 1929-1939*, by Pierre Berton

Remnants (A Fable)

— • — Act I — • —

I. i. A street in shtetl Luzniki, eastern Poland, 1925.

> *JOSEPH sits in the square, lost in thought. JUDAH and*
> *REUBEN, his brothers, enter. REUBEN holds a letter.*

JUDAH
Look, it's the little shit.

REUBEN
Never mind him. Listen to this – it's addressed to the old man, from Uncle Sol.

(reading the letter) "Dear Brother, New York is a bustling... a bustling" – what's this word? It's English.

JUDAH
(with an accent) Metropolis.

REUBEN
"Metropolis. I would be happy, dear brother, to support any one of your boys, if only you would send me one – or three, or all twelve! America is not nearly as terrible a place as you all thought. A man can not only make money, he can keep it, too. They really love freedom here. Why, a man can even vote to put another man in office – and his vote really means something! The women are not so beautiful as ours, that's a bad thing; but there are no pogroms here, either. I send you a steamship ticket, so that you might send me a single one of your children. Jacob, my brother, I miss you dearly. Write soon." *(holds up the ticket)*

JUDAH
Burn it. Burn that ticket and burn that goddamn letter. Nobody's going anywhere. The old man'd cut off his left arm before he let a single one of his sons go. Screwed our mother to death to fill his shop with cheap labour. And there sits the seed of his union with the little whore who took her place. Joseph.

REUBEN
Don't waste your time. The others are waiting for us.

JUDAH
Joseph.

JOSEPH
Hello, Judah.

JUDAH
"Hello, Judah." Why aren't you at yeshiva, learning to split talmudic hairs?

JOSEPH
I'm thinking about something.

JUDAH
What?

JOSEPH
I can't tell you.

JUDAH
Why not? Is it something only the wise ones understand? Do you think we're too stupid to help you with it?

JOSEPH
It isn't the kind of thing you can help me with.

JUDAH
You hear that, Reuben? He thinks we're idiots.

JOSEPH
I didn't say that.

JUDAH
He thinks because we work and sweat all day long, stitching, sewing, cutting, dying, on our feet, while he, he, sits on a bench, hunched over, muttering irrelevant prayers, that he's better than us, smarter than us, more important than us – Oh but don't leave us, Joseph, it's a mitzvah to converse with the less fortunate.

JOSEPH
Leave me alone.

JUDAH
Get back here, yeshiva boy, and tell us what you were thinking.

JOSEPH
You won't like it.

JUDAH
Now he's telling us what we think. That's very New Testament. Do you know something, Reuben, I think yeshiva boy's been reading the words of Christ.

REUBEN
Come on, Judah, we need to talk.

JUDAH

You talk. I want yeshiva boy to tell me what he's thinking. Tell us. Tell us. Tell us.

JUDAH twists JOSEPH's arm behind his back.

JOSEPH

Ow! You're hurting me!

REUBEN

Leave him alone.

JUDAH

Tell me what you're thinking, yeshiva boy, or I'll twist your goddamn arm like the hairs of those black-hatted yids.

JOSEPH

Alright, alright.

REUBEN

Let him go.

JUDAH

Little yid better learn to fight for himself. Now what is this deep thought you're thinking?

JOSEPH

It's not a thought. It's a dream.

JUDAH

Oh, "a dream." So that's what he does in yeshiva all day – he sleeps. After all, a man can't dream unless he's asleep. Hey, I ought to be a talmudist, thinking deep thoughts like that.

REUBEN

Alright, Joseph, tell us so we can be on our way.

JOSEPH

We were in the shop, making clothes.

JUDAH

Who was?

JOSEPH

All of us – you, me, our brothers, and Father. Suddenly the suits you were working on rose up, as though there were people in them. They surrounded me, and bowed down.

Beat.

JUDAH

You think we bow down to you?

REUBEN
Judah.

JUDAH
We bow down to you?

REUBEN
Alright, Joseph. Go to shul. Go.

JOSEPH
I said you wouldn't like it.

JOSEPH goes.

JUDAH
Why'd you stop me? I'd have wrung his neck.

REUBEN
Yes. I believe you would have. And gained what? You've already cemented your reputation.

JUDAH
Let's have the letter.

REUBEN hands over the letter. JUDAH lights it on fire.

REUBEN
I think you've gone mad.

JUDAH
No, sir. Born that way.

I. ii. Luzniki. Synagogue.

The family, in synagogue. JOSEPH and BENJAMIN, at back, speak beneath the chanting of kaddish.

JOSEPH
Benjamin, you're mad at me, aren't you?

BENJAMIN shrugs.

Oh, you're a fine one for shrugging. Listen. You think I want to go away to yeshiva? It wasn't my idea, I can tell you that. But Father insisted, says the best teacher is in Vilnius, and–

JACOB casts a glance back. JOSEPH prays.

You're gonna get me in trouble, little brother. Listen. Vilnius isn't so far. I'll be back for holidays, and maybe once or twice you could come and visit.

BENJAMIN shrugs.

Benjamin, that's why I had the dream.

BENJAMIN shrugs.

It means we'll always be together. You'll always be with me, no matter where I go. But it also means I have to go. Who knows? Maybe I'll become a great scholar—Reb Dubczanski!—sought out for my interpretations.

JACOB looks back. JOSEPH prays again.

Adon Olam begins.

CONGREGATION
Adon olam, asher malach...

JOSEPH
I'll send for you. Is it a deal, or what?

BENJAMIN shrugs. Then playfully smacks JOSEPH on the back.

Okay, I guess it's a deal.

JOSEPH joins the others in the song.

CONGREGATION
  ...b'terem kol y'tzir nivra...

I. iii. Luzniki. Home of the Dubczanski family.

JUDAH, with PISCHUK, the shabbes goy, who prepares the table.

JUDAH
(sings to the tune of Adon Olam) "For a tailor to work a whole week was his goal/and for this his reward was a bagel with a hole."
(to PISCHUK) What do you think of my song, Pischuk?

PISCHUK
It's a good song, Master Judah, I suppose.

JUDAH
Tell me Pischuk, do you like working for Jews?

PISCHUK
I don't mind, as long as you pay.

JUDAH
What do we pay, Pischuk?

PISCHUK
Ten *zlotys* a week.

JUDAH

That much, eh? Does that buy you much meat? Or drink? It sure as hell isn't gonna buy you your farm, is it? Have you got kids, Pischuk?

PISCHUK

Kids? No.

JUDAH

How about a wife?

PISCHUK

It's not that I don't enjoy talking to you, Master Judah, but if you don't mind, I have to finish up before the others get home from evening prayers.

JUDAH

Yes, Pischuk, you go ahead. I'd help out, of course, but my religion forbids me from working on the sabbath.

PISCHUK

It also commands you to pray.

JUDAH

Yes, but you know, these days prayer is a form of work. It's a contradiction I can't quite get my head around. *(sings)* "For a tailor to work a whole week was his goal...." Do you know something, Pischuk? My father, the greatest tailor in all of Poland, or at least in this part of Poland, or let's just say in our little shtetl – well, my father saves every scrap of cloth from every garment that he makes. He offers these scraps to his clients, all of whom, naturally, refuse to take them. And do you know why my father offers these scraps, dear Pischuk? I'll tell you. As proof that he observed the commandment as laid down in Genesis: "Not even one thread have I taken from them." *(beat)* "Not even one thread." This same man who pays slave wages to his tailors and seamstresses; who treats his sons—all but one—as little more than slaves; this same man will go to his grave convinced that he has fulfilled God's commandments.

PISCHUK

If you please, Master Judah.

JUDAH

I don't please, Pischuk. And don't call me "Master" you wretched Pole. I hate to see a man choke back bile on my account. "If you please." I please nothing. And nothing, and no one, pleases me. I was born a Jew in a country that hates the Jew; and, as I am hated, so I hate. I hate the Christian for hating the Jew, and

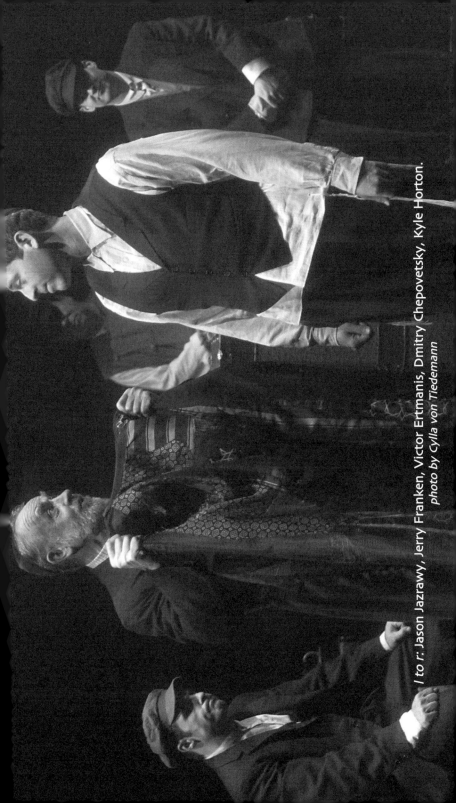

l to r: Jason Jazrawy, Jerry Franken, Victor Ertmanis, Dmitry Chepovetsky, Kyle Horton.

photo by Cylla von Tiedemann

I hate the Jew for being hated. I hear the hoofbeats, my friend, pounding into the soil. Those hoofbeats are coming for me. And you, dear Pischuk, will assist in the slaughter. *(pause; sings:)* "For a tailor to work a whole week was his goal; and for this his reward was a bagel with a hole."

JACOB, REUBEN and SIMON enter.

REUBEN
Well, Father, if you ask me, it's just a lot of talk.

JACOB
Let me catch them, that's all. I only pray to God to let me catch them.

JUDAH
Catch who?

JACOB
Bundists!

JUDAH
In our fair shtetl?

JACOB
Trying to unionise my shop? I'll break their necks with my own hands!

JUDAH
Not those hands!

JACOB
These hands!

JUDAH
Now, Father, what would make you think there are Bundists in our midst?

JACOB
I hear things. I hear plenty. And none of it good. A man works for years – years! He scrapes, he saves–

JUDAH
I'm sure there's music for this.

JACOB
And what's his reward? Communists!

SIMON
But, Father–

JACOB
Simon, was I speaking to you?

SIMON

No, Father.

JACOB

Stay out of things you know nothing about.

SIMON

Yes, Father.

JACOB

Which is to say, most things.

REUBEN

Father, these rumours. I wouldn't put any stock in them.

JACOB

You wouldn't, huh?

JUDAH

Where did you hear such things?

JACOB

Oh I hear, my boy. I hear plenty. And none of it good. But it's shabbes, and nearly Yom Kippur, so I'm willing to forgive, so long as these heathens keep their godless ideas out of my shop.

JUDAH

Forgive and forget – the Dubczanski way. No, wait, it's forgive and forget you forgave, I always get it mixed up.

JACOB

Keep talking, I'll give you something to forget. But where are Joseph and Benjamin? Simon, go find Joseph.

JUDAH

Fetch, boy, woof!

JACOB

Hurry, hurry. Pischuk, get me the package, the one I showed you. Leave that challah, Judah. Suddenly his stomach's not so sore.

JUDAH

My quiet hours of reflection here were all the balm I needed.

JACOB

Next time, you can reflect in shul, with the rest of us. Listen, I took a big order today. The Polish officer Oustrovski – you know him?

JUDAH

He of the little poodle?

JACOB
Just the one. He likes my tailoring, and why not, he's a man of great taste. While the other shops churn out ready-mades, we provide clothes to last a lifetime. Oustrovski ordered suits and gowns for the officers and their wives. The thing is, he needs them in two weeks.

JUDAH
That's impossible.

JACOB
Not in my shop. Tomorrow, you'll go to Vilnius to pick up the material.

REUBEN
On shabbes?

JACOB
It's an emergency. God provides for such things. Go after sundown.

JUDAH
We have so many orders to fill as it is.

REUBEN
One more won't kill us.

JACOB
And you'll take Joseph. I want he should see the city.

SIMON returns, with JOSEPH and BENJAMIN.

There he is – my boy! My boy! You know, it never fails, it doesn't matter how low I might be feeling, how sad, or upset, but when I see this boy, this angel, my mood lifts right away! Come, put your arms around me, let me kiss you. God looks over you, because you were a gift to me in my old age. And you, too, Benjamin; only God, for reasons only he himself knows, took my beloved Rachela from me, twelve years ago, in exchange for you. –Well, where's the package? Give it to me, Pischuk, give, give. Now, before we have dinner, I want to give you something, Joseph, my angel, my beloved. Open, open.

As JOSEPH opens the package:

JUDAH
What's the occasion?

JACOB
The occasion is it's finished.

JOSEPH lifts the coat from the package.

JACOB
Nu?

JOSEPH
It's beautiful.

JACOB
Of course it's beautiful. What else would it be when I made it with my own hands? Here, here, let me help you. It's the latest style, I saw it in on the great Rebbe of Vilnius, I said, "That's for my Joseph, I'll make it for him myself." See, there's extra material on the cuffs, so when you should be older, you'll just extend it. Well, we'll have to let it out a bit now, I see. You're growing so fast. But this coat, my boy, this coat will last all your life, you'll have it on your travels, always, wherever you go! Nu? Who loves my coat?

JUDAH
A rare gift, Father. And to think, he's already had his bar mitzvah.

REUBEN
Very elegant.

SIMON
Can I have one?

JACOB
"Can you have one?" Go find your brain where you dropped it, I'll make you two. Now look. Look, on the inside. See what's in here? The lining! The lining! It's made from the scraps of garments I've made for my customers. I've been saving them, so when my time comes, I should be buried with them, as proof that not one–

JUDAH
(overlapping) –That not one single thread have I taken from them.

JACOB
That's right.

JUDAH
Only now you've turned your burial cloth into a coat.

JACOB
For my Joseph. Who is speechless.

JUDAH
It runs in that part of the family.

JACOB slaps JUDAH.

JACOB
Not one more word. Not one. Come. Joseph, tonight you'll say the baruch'a over the bread. Come!

JACOB goes, followed by JOSEPH and BENJAMIN.

JUDAH
Your duties are over, Pischuk.

PISCHUK
Yes, Master Judah. Goodnight, then.

PISCHUK goes. JOSEPH is heard saying the baruch'a.

SIMON
Does the old man know it's us?

JUDAH
Lower your voice.

REUBEN
He couldn't. If he did, we'd know it.

JUDAH
Of course he knows. What do you think all that "forgive and forget" crap was about? Well, we're screwed now, aren't we?

REUBEN
For a time. We'll lay low.

JUDAH
How much lower do you think we can get?

SIMON
I say forget it. I say to hell with the shop, the union, this town. There's no future for us here. I say we march in there right now, look the old man straight in the face and say, "We want to go to Palestine."

JUDAH
Palestine. Yeah, they could use a mule like you.

JACOB
(off) Reuben! Simon!

REUBEN
Coming! Are you coming? –What is it?

JUDAH
It's Joseph. He's the one who's ratting on us.

REUBEN
We don't know that.

JUDAH
Why's he been hanging around the shop lately?

REUBEN
Father said he wanted him to learn the trade.

JUDAH
No, no. Little dreamer's spying on us.

SIMON
He's right. I know he's right.

REUBEN
You have no proof.

JUDAH
We just saw it, stitched together by the old man himself.

BENJAMIN returns.

What do you want, mute?

BENJAMIN mimes eating.

We're coming. Go away.

BENJAMIN mimes farting at them. Goes.

We'll meet tonight. All the others, as well. Everyone has to be in on this.

REUBEN
What are you thinking?

JUDAH
I'm not thinking.

I. iv. A road through the forest.

The next night. JUDAH, REUBEN, SIMON and JOSEPH. A horse-and-buggy is heard, off. JUDAH holds the horse whip.

JUDAH
Brr. Goddamn cold out, eh boys? We'll stop here and eat.

JOSEPH
Shouldn't we go on? Father needs the material right away.

JUDAH
Look, dreamer. Vilnius is another twenty miles. The horses need to rest, eat and drink. And so do I.

He pulls out a flask.

JOSEPH
You've been drinking since we left.

JUDAH
Not really! Reuben, do you hear that? I've been drinking since we left.

REUBEN
Let's get on with this.

JUDAH
Where are the others?

JOSEPH
What's going on?

REUBEN
They'll be along in a minute.

JOSEPH
We should keep going. Father said to–

JUDAH
"Father said, Father said" – Father's not here, is he?

JOSEPH
Someone's coming.

SIMON
It's Pischuk.

JUDAH
So it is.

JOSEPH
Pischuk? What's he doing out here?

JUDAH
We'll ask him when he gets here. *(beat)* Joseph, we have a question for you. Why have you been hanging out at the shop lately?

SIMON
You deaf? Answer him.

JOSEPH
Father wants me to learn the trade.

JUDAH
Really. Have you learned much?

JOSEPH
A little.

clockwise from top right:
Alon Nashman, Alex Poch-Goldin, Dmitry Chepovetsky, Jason Jazrawy.
photo by Cylla von Tiedemann

JUDAH
A little. Well, tell us, what's the first thing an apprentice tailor learns? –Dreamer, I'm talking to you.

REUBEN
Pischuk's getting closer. I see another wagon now. It's the others.

JOSEPH
I don't understand. Is Father sending everyone?

JUDAH
Who said you could ask questions? What's the first thing a tailor learns to do?

JOSEPH
Well, to – well, how to sew.

JUDAH
Ah, "how to sew." That's a good one, eh Simon? Well, guess what, Dreamer – you're right! That's exactly what a tailor learns to do first. To be specific, he learns how to sew a buttonhole.

JUDAH pulls a shirt and a sewing kit from his bag, hands them to JOSEPH.

At least, that's the first thing I learned to do. I was twelve. It took me a while to get it. You're much older. Why don't you show us how well you've been learning your new trade?

JOSEPH just stares at the material.

Don't be shy, Dreamer. You, who excels at everything – you could probably teach us a thing or two.

JOSEPH
(quietly) I don't know how.

JUDAH
What's that?

JOSEPH
I don't know how.

SIMON
You see?

REUBEN
Alright.

JUDAH
Well, then, Dreamer, what have you been learning in that shop? What have you been doing?

JUDAH slaps JOSEPH, hard, to the ground.

Little shit!

REUBEN

Don't do that!

JUDAH

Liar! Pick him up.

> *SIMON yanks JOSEPH to his knees, holding the whip against his throat.*

You've been spying on us, haven't you, Dreamer? Haven't you?

JOSEPH

No...

JUDAH

Telling the old man about us.

JOSEPH

No, I didn't... I wouldn't...

> *SIMON chokes JOSEPH hard.*

No! Please!

REUBEN

Judah, that's enough. Simon.

JUDAH

Little shit! We should kill you. We should kill you.

> *Enter PISCHUK.*

PISCHUK

Let him go. What are you doing? Let him go!

> *PISCHUK pulls JOSEPH free.*

It's alright. Can you stand?

JUDAH

Never mind. Take him away, Pischuk. Take him and throw him into a pit. Put a rock over the pit so that no light gets in.

REUBEN

Stop talking like that, Judah. Give him the ticket.

JUDAH

Into a pit, I say!

REUBEN

The ticket.

JUDAH

(handing over the steamship ticket) Go ahead.

REUBEN takes the ticket, hands it to PISCHUK.

REUBEN
Everything's set?

PISCHUK
Yes, yes.

REUBEN
You have the papers? There's his trunk.

PISCHUK
Yes.

JOSEPH
What's happening? What are you doing?

REUBEN
You're going away, Joseph.

JOSEPH
Away?

REUBEN
To America.

JOSEPH
America?

REUBEN
Quiet. Just be happy we didn't kill you. We should have, for what you did. They all wanted to. I talked them out of it, do you understand? Because I didn't want your blood on our hands. Go on, Joseph.

JOSEPH
Don't send me away. Father... Benjamin...

REUBEN
Pischuk.

JOSEPH
I want to see Benjamin. He needs me.

SIMON
We'll take care of Benjamin.

PISCHUK
We'd better go. There's just enough time.

JUDAH
Take him. And don't think about trying to come back, Joseph. If I ever see you again, I will kill you. But first Benjamin, and make you watch.

JOSEPH
I've done nothing. Nothing.

JUDAH
Of course you have. You were born.

JOSEPH
Please. I swear to God.

JUDAH
Yes. Well you stick with God. We'll stick with the Bund. Now the coat.

JOSEPH
Please, no...

JUDAH
Give me that goddamn thing.

JUDAH takes the coat, grabs a sharp instrument from his bag.

Of course it's customary, when a member of the family dies, to rip a piece of clothing.

Rips the coat; bounds and gags JOSEPH.

REUBEN
Not too tight. Easy. You're hurting him.

JUDAH pushes REUBEN away, finishes. PISCHUK leads JOSEPH away.

JUDAH
Oh – Joseph! I almost forgot! *(gets to his knees, bows deeply)* Goodbye, Dreamer.

PISCHUK takes JOSEPH off. JUDAH turns to REUBEN.

Hit me.

REUBEN
Hit you? But–

JUDAH hits REUBEN. SIMON joins in. They brawl.

I. v. Dubczanski shop.

JACOB at work; REUBEN, SIMON and JUDAH go to him.

JACOB
You're back early.

Silence. JACOB looks at them, sizes them up.

What happened?

JUDAH

We were in the forest... men on horseback, fifteen of them, attacked us...

JACOB

Where is Joseph?

JUDAH

We fought them best we could, but with no weapons, what could we do?

JACOB

Where is he? Where is he?

JUDAH

Father, they took him. They made us sit, and watch, as they tied him by the hands to one of their horses... I watched as one man lifted his arm, holding a strap, and, saying, "this is what happens to Jews," brought the strap down on the horse, which galloped away, dragging Joseph behind. Father, he cried for you, he cried, he cried, until we could no longer hear his screams. They stole our money, and left us the horses, so that we could bring back word. We searched for Joseph, but could find no sign of him, no sign but this. *(presents JOSEPH's torn and tattered coat)* Here, you see, his blood, Father. The blood of your son.

JACOB

(cradling the coat) Joseph, my Joseph. Lost, lost, lost. I was promised a multitude, and now it's been taken. God gave you to me, beautiful boy, so I could look upon you in the hour of my death, and close my eyes on wisdom and beauty. Now these godless ones have taken you from me, and my eyes have nothing to see, no, nothing more to see.

REUBEN

Father–

JACOB

Go out, find me these men, find me one, a single one of them, bring them here to me, let me cut him to a thousand pieces, here, here, here!... My Joseph... my Joseph... there never was, and never will be, one so precious... do you hear me, my Joseph... my Joseph...

I. vi. Road to Vilnius.

PISCHUK and JOSEPH.

PISCHUK

So you're up. You slept. Long time. We'll soon be at the train station. From there to Gdansk, and the steamer.

JOSEPH

You're coming with?

PISCHUK

I'm to make sure you get on the ship. *(shoves some food at him)* Eat. I packed some food in your trunk. You watch that trunk, do you understand? Sit on it night and day. Take it with you everywhere. Drag it with you. Maybe you'll meet someone on the ship, he'll pretend to be your friend, but he won't be your friend. He'll say, "Go on, go take a piss, I'll watch your things." And when you come back, your things will be gone, you won't see the little thief again.

JOSEPH

Pischuk, take me back. My father will pay you, only take me back.

PISCHUK

I've been well paid. Your brothers saw to that. There's money for you, too. Your brothers, they have a conscience. I heard them arguing over what to do with you. Judah was the most outspoken. He didn't say he wanted to kill you, but he made it clear that's what he wanted, and Simon, dumb as he is, brutal as he is, he offered to break your neck himself. The others said nothing. They're no better than a mob, the others. Except Reuben, you see. Reuben was the one who came up with the idea. "Send him to America," he said. "He'll be out of the way, then, and we'll never hear from him again." No, Joseph, you're better off going away, you'll see.

JOSEPH

Let me go, Pischuk. Let me go, let me go.

PISCHUK

My father beat me every chance he got. He was a stinking drunk, you know, he made nothing of his life. Every time the door slammed shut and we heard his heavy footsteps, our blood ran cold and we'd look for a place to hide. I'd put my arm around my sister, only she couldn't stop shivering. And in the dark there of our hiding place, we could hear him, calling, "Come out, or I'll feed you to the Jews." I said to myself, "Please God help me.

Please don't let him find us, God. I'll be good if only you don't
let him find us." But he always did, Master Joseph. So why is it,
do you suppose, that I kept on asking God to help me? ...Look.
I have something to give you. I've seen the other Jews do it,
when their sons go away. *(hands JOSEPH a photo)* Your father and
mother. You're supposed to put it on the wall by your bed. To
guide you.

I. vii. Halifax, Nova Scotia. Pier 21 – Canadian Immigration.

> *Two weeks later. JOSEPH stands in a long line of immigrants
> waiting to be processed. An IMMIGRATION OFFICER sits
> at a table. [Note: dialogue between square brackets indicates that
> characters are speaking a language other than English with one
> another.]*

INSPECTOR
Immigrants to Canada! Have your bags ready for inspection! All
bags will be searched!

IMMIGRATION OFFICER
(to JOSEPH) You. You there. Step forward. You speak English?
(to someone in line) Hey, step back there, folks.

PERSON IN LINE
Pushing, pushing.

2ND PERSON IN LINE
[Idiot, you stepped on my bag.]

3RD PERSON IN LINE
[So don't put it in front of my foot.]

IMMIGRATION OFFICER
Just stay behind the line. Things'll go a lot faster if you people'd
just – forget it. *(to JOSEPH)* Alright, what's your name? Your
name?

> *JOSEPH shows him papers.*

What's a matter, cat got your tongue? *(looking over the papers)*
Joseph Dub – Dob– *(sighs)* No, that won't do. Let's see, you're
from uhh... Luzniki. Joseph Luzniki. That's not much better. Ah,
your father's a tailor. *(miming)* Tailor? Right. *(writes down)* Joseph
Taylor. *(keeps looking through papers)* Hey, wait a second. Says here
you're supposed to go to New York. New York. This is Halifax.
Canada.

MAX
Mister, he don't speak.

IMMIGRATION OFFICER
Huh? You with him? Come here.

PERSON IN LINE
Hey!

IMMIGRATION OFFICER
Quiet. *(to MAX)* You know this guy? You related?

MAX
Maybe.

IMMIGRATION OFFICER
What do you mean, maybe?

MAX
Who knows? Go back far enough, all are related.

IMMIGRATION OFFICER
Look, wise guy, we've got a thousand people to process, we're short-staffed, and I was called into work on my daughter's birthday. Do I look happy? Now if you've got something useful to say, say it.

MAX
On ship, he don't say nothing. Two weeks, like this. *(buttons his lip)* Pray, pray, pray, day and night, all he do is pray. He's ehhhh student, okay? Yeshiva boy.

IMMIGRATION OFFICER
What's that?

MAX
Yeshiva. Like ehhhh – university.

IMMIGRATION OFFICER
Is that what he came over to do? Study?

MAX
I don't know. Ask him.

IMMIGRATION OFFICER
You said he doesn't speak.

MAX
So don't ask.

PERSON IN LINE
Come on, come on, six hours we are waiting.

IMMIGRATION OFFICER
(to MAX) Ask him why he got off the boat.

MAX whispers. JOSEPH whispers back.

Not so dumb after all, huh?

MAX
He say he's afraid to go to New York.

IMMIGRATION OFFICER
Afraid of what?

MAX whispers; JOSEPH whispers.

MAX
He say he is orphan, has uncle in New York, but bad man, will beat him.

OFFICER looks JOSEPH over.

IMMIGRATION OFFICER
Ask him if he's a Communist.

MAX
Him? Mister, you're joking.

IMMIGRATION OFFICER
I'll let you know if I'm joking.

MAX
Mister, look. Boy is religious student, okay? All he knows is to pray. I show you. I get him to do the shma. Very holy prayer.

MAX whispers in JOSEPH's ear.

JOSEPH
Shma Yisroel, adonai–

MAX
Okay, is good. See? No way he is Communist. Communists don't believe in such things. Look at him. You think this boy is going to start revolution? Is against Jewish religion to believe in communism.

IMMIGRATION OFFICER
Well how come so many Communists are Jews?

MAX
Okay, but those are not good Jews. Mister, I tell you what. Let boy come with me. I bring him to farm. All of us from ship, we are going to farm. Gimli, Manitoba. You know? Work farm, cluck cluck, chick chick. Build muscles. Good Canadians. We walk around, "hm, very interesting." Boy is young, strong.

IMMIGRATION OFFICER

I don't know.

MAX

Exactly, you don't know, so I'm telling you. Look, you have information for me. Okay, here is my papers. I will be boy's ehhhhh – I watch out for him, okay? He do something bad, you send me back. He have money.

IMMIGRATION OFFICER

What's that?

MAX

For train ticket. *(whispers in JOSEPH's ear; JOSEPH presents wad of bills; MAX shoves the bills at the OFFICER)* American cash. I see him counting it on ship. Not too bright this boy. How much it take to buy ticket? You count.

> *Pause. OFFICER counts the money, pockets half, gives the rest back.*

IMMIGRATION OFFICER

That oughta be enough.

MAX

Okay, mister. Get daughter nice present, okay?

IMMIGRATION OFFICER

Get outta here before I change my mind. And tell him to stay on that farm. That way he's happy. I'm happy. Everybody's happy. Next.

I. viii. Train.

> *MAX and JOSEPH board train. MAX is laughing.*

MAX

Oh, that was beautiful, Joe, wasn't it?

JOSEPH

(overlapping with MAX) Why did you do that? Why did you do that?

MAX

Wasn't that beautiful? I knew the guy would go for it, I knew it. These Canadians, they're as corrupt as they come, only in a nice way.

JOSEPH

Why did you do that?

MAX
What, bribe the guy? I didn't see any other way out of it for you kid. He thought you were a Communist. We gotta help each other. Name's Max, Max Becker. Used to be Novgorodnik – I fixed it.

CONDUCTOR
All aboard!

MAX
Here we go. Hey, kid, you ever heard a Jewish cow? A Jewish cow? Nuuuuuuu? – Listen, when we get to Toronto, first thing we gotta do, we gotta go to this place, United Bakers Dairy, it's a restaurant. My cousin wrote me all about it.

JOSEPH
Toronto?

MAX
Yeah.

JOSEPH
You said Manitoba.

MAX
Yeah. Uh, kid what are you gonna do on a farm? Huh? Seriously. You don't know from farming. You're a shtetl kid. Your dad was a tailor, right? That's what the man said? Okay. Good. So we'll get us a couple jobs in the needle trade. They can use guys like us. You can sew a buttonhole, can't you? Kid, you ever hear of Karl Marx? Karl Marx? Well, Karl Marx...

Train sounds increase, drowning out MAX's speech. Hours later.

(yawning) And that's why it's important that *(yawning)* Scuse me – we keep fighting for better conditions... Joe? Joe, you sleeping?

CONDUCTOR
Tickets... tickets, please...

MAX
(handing over his ticket) Joseph? Wake up. Your ticket. The man needs your ticket.

JOSEPH
(searching) I can't find it.

MAX
You drop it?

l to r: Jerry Franken, Alon Nashman, Victor Ertmanis, Dmitry Chepovetsky, Jason Jazrawy, Alex Poch-Goldin.
photo by Cylla von Tiedemann

JOSEPH
I don't know. It was here, in this pocket.

JUDAH
Here you are, Joseph. Here's your ticket.

JOSEPH
Thank you, Judah. Simon?

SIMON
You have to be more careful with your things, Joseph.

JOSEPH
Yes, Simon, I will. Are you all here? Asher... Daniel... Levi...

REUBEN
Give the man your ticket, Joseph. He's waiting.

JOSEPH
Reuben. *(hands ticket to CONDUCTOR)* Here you are.

CONDUCTOR
Very good. *(gently touches JOSEPH's face)* Very good.

JOSEPH
But where's–? Isn't Benjamin with you?

JUDAH
Oh, he's fine, Joseph, fine.

REUBEN
Yes, no need to worry about Benjamin.

JOSEPH
But where is he?

CONDUCTOR
(discretely) Joseph. Come along. This way. This way. I'll show you.
Tickets, please. Tickets.

They make their way down the car. A man is sobbing.

Why, what's the matter, man?

CRYING MAN
Oh, sir. My sons. Murdered, all of them, murdered, their remains
scattered there in the fields for the dogs.

CONDUCTOR
Dear, dear. Tell us what happened.

CRYING MAN
Wolves. A pack of them, attacked us.

CONDUCTOR
Joseph, why do you stand there? See if you can find Benjamin.

CRYING MAN
I watched them rip my children to pieces, limbs torn from bodies, flesh ripped from bones, blood soaking the ground.

JOSEPH
Benjamin?

CRYING MAN
My own children, and I couldn't help them.

JOSEPH
Benjamin? ...Benjamin...

BENJAMIN
(calling out) Jooooseph.

JOSEPH
There you are.

BENJAMIN
It's a good hiding place, isn't it?

JOSEPH
You're talking.

BENJAMIN
Joseph. You're going to meet a man who will save you. You have to go with him. If you don't go with him, you'll never see me again. He'll lead you to me. I'm gonna hide again now. Ready?

CONDUCTOR
Back to your seats, folks... Union Station next. Union Station. Come along, fella. *(seats him)* This your stop?

MAX
Joseph... Joseph.... The man needs to see your ticket.

> *JOSEPH hands over the ticket. Puts his hand to his throat. Starts to cough.*

What is it?

CONDUCTOR
He alright?

MAX
Joe, you want some water?

> *JOSEPH's cough worsens. Locusts fly out of his mouth.*

Locusts!

CONDUCTOR

Hold him down. Cover his mouth. Cover it!

MAX

Joe! Joe!

JOSEPH sits up, blinking awake.

Sorry, kid. You were gagging in your sleep. You okay? Didn't mean to... it's just, the man wants to see your ticket.

JOSEPH

Yes. It's here. *(hands it over)*

CONDUCTOR

Gimli. Going to the farm, I see. Lot of you boys on this train. *(starts off)* Toronto, next stop... Union Station...

MAX

Well, Joe. This is it. You with me? Come on. We'll do some things.

The train sounds continue... then begin to merge with the sound of sewing machines... hundreds of sewing machines...

I. ix. Pottinger & Sons. The cutting room.

Men at their stations.

MAX

(above the cacophony of machines) Joe! Joe! You coming tonight, Joe?

JOSEPH doesn't answer.

Everyone's gonna be there, Joe! Important meeting.

JOSEPH indicates he can't hear.

Tim Buck's gonna be there, Joe! Tim Buck! I know you can hear me!

Mr. POTTINGER comes along, inspecting the work.

Hello, Mr. Pottinger.

POTTINGER nods. Bell rings for end of shift. The machines are turned off.

Mr. Pottinger – brings you to cutting room?

POTTINGER

Oh, just – well – thought I'd take a look at the new pattern. Very nice, isn't it? Joseph designed this one. Said he saw it in Vilnius.

That's going to make a fine coat. Hm. *(beat)* How's Mrs. Becker, then, Max?

MAX
She is well, Mr. Pottinger, thank you.

POTTINGER
Well don't let me keep you from her. Or the children. Very important. Very important.

> *When POTTINGER turns his back, MAX indicates that the old man's breath stinks from drink.*

Oh, Joseph, may I have a word? Er, about the – new design.

JOSEPH
Okay, Mr. Pottinger.

MAX
[Joe, I'll see you at the meeting, right?]

POTTINGER
Oh no no no. English only in here, boys, English only! I-I-I hate to be the enforcer but, a rule's a rule.

MAX
Sorry, Mr. Pottinger, was only saying to Joseph we will wait for him at diner. Wife and kids. Going to United Dairy.

POTTINGER
Oh, that's fine. I used to eat there.

MAX
Goodnight, Mr. Pottinger.

> *MAX goes.*

POTTINGER
Well, Joseph, I... I want to talk to you about...

JOSEPH
The new design, Mr. Pottinger?

POTTINGER
No, no. No no no. The new design is wonderful. You've quite an eye there, Joseph – quite two eyes, when you get right down to it. I, I, really think you have a future there, Joseph, yes I do. I can't offer you a position on the design floor immediately, you understand, I – no, things are tightening up considerably, Joseph, I – this darned economic situation, it's...

> *Pulls out a bottle of Seagram's whiskey.*

Would you like some, Joseph?

JOSEPH
No, thank you.

POTTINGER
Oh do. Do do do.

JOSEPH takes a shot.

That's the boy. –Yes, these are... interesting times. –But with a
new Prime Minister, who knows? Maybe Bennett can find a way
to get things moving again; Mackenzie King, he never lifted a
finger to help the rest of us, the stinking hypocrite, him with all
his money and power. It's all the same to you, I suppose. That's
fine. But a man like me, I have to think about these things. Yes,
I do. Orders are drying up. One look at the balance sheet tells
me, it's not good. Not good at all. Then there's the unions – well.
I can't even keep up with them. International Ladies in one
corner; the Cloakmakers in another; and me, caught in the
middle. Oh, but I'm the boss, so if I resist their demands, I'm
the bad one. The big bad wolf.

*POTTINGER fills his lungs and—standing among the
machinery—blows out, a la the big bad wolf.*

JOSEPH
Mr. Pottinger, I–

POTTINGER
Joseph, how long have you been working for me? Four years, isn't
it?

JOSEPH
Four years, six months, twelve days.

POTTINGER
And in—is that right?—in all that time, have I once asked you
to do something that wasn't in your... your... heart? *(beat)* Joseph,
I want you to do something for me. I want you to get on your
knees.

JOSEPH
My knees?

POTTINGER
Your knees, Joseph. And pray.

POTTINGER gets to his knees; brings JOSEPH with him.

Joseph, I know you're being tempted, tempted by these unions.
Do you think I'm blind? Deaf? I know what goes on here.
There's something brewing, and that Max Becker, he's the one

with his hands over the cauldron. Oh, my boy, don't drink their poison. They're godless, these men. They believe in nothing. They want only to destroy. We must stand firm against them. Pray with me, Joseph. The Lord's Prayer. Surely you've heard of it. "Our Father, who art in heaven." It's like the shma. "Our Father, who art in heaven..."

JOSEPH

Mr. Pottinger, don't ask me to do this.

POTTINGER

"Hallowed be thy name..."

JOSEPH

Mr. Pottinger, listen to me.

POTTINGER

"Give us this day, our daily bread..."

JOSEPH

You have been so kind to me, Mr. Pottinger.

POTTINGER

"Forgive us our trespasses..."

JOSEPH

But I can't do this.

POTTINGER

"As we forgive those who trespass against us..."

JOSEPH

I cannot pretend to be something other than what I am.

POTTINGER

"And lead us not into–" *(having heard JOSEPH)* Why not?

JOSEPH

He will be angry with me.

POTTINGER

(pointing up) All the more reason to pray to Him.

JOSEPH

Not God – my father. He would not understand.

POTTINGER

Oh, you wonderful boy. To love a father so.

JOSEPH

Mr. Pottinger: I am Jewish. You know I am Jewish.

Pause.

POTTINGER
As was I. Yes. Me. Lewis Pottinger; aka, Lewis Putzinger. Try
making your way through the world with a name like that, my
boy. So I changed it. Changed everything. What else was I to
do? If I wanted to stay in this country, and rise, I would have to
pretend to be one of them. If I wanted my children to do well,
go to university, become a doctor, a lawyer, to walk down the
street with their heads held high, I would have to make this
sacrifice. The children were too young to understand. That was
a blessing. Thirty years I've kept that secret. So many secrets.

*They are face to face. POTTINGER suddenly leaps at JOSEPH,
trying to kiss him.*

JOSEPH
Mr. Pottinger!

POTTINGER
Oh God forgive me. Forgive me, Joseph. Beautiful boy. Come
here, Joseph. Joseph.

*POTTINGER chases JOSEPH around the machines, which topple
over.*

Get back here. Little tempter. Four years, six months, twelve
days – I've been counting too! I've kept myself away from you.
Well I can't keep myself away anymore – and it's all your fault,
your fault, you little tempter.

JOSEPH
Stop it, Mr. Pottinger. Stop it! Stop it!

The night watchman enters.

POTTINGER
Well don't just stand there – it's sabotage! He's destroying the
machines! He's a Red! A Red! A Red and a Jew! Get out! Get
out! Get out of my shop!

JOSEPH runs off.

I. x. Park. A bench.

JOSEPH runs on, out of breath.

BROWNSHIRTS
(*off, singing:*) Oh, give me a home, where the white man can roam,
and the Jews, wops and bohunks don't play/Where seldom is
heard a disgusting Yid word/And the Reds are forbidden to stay.

> *JOSEPH looks in horror as the men approach. He hides. The gang enters.*

FIRST BROWNSHIRT
I nailed him! Pushed his fuckin nose into his brain.

SECOND BROWNSHIRT
The first victory in the noble war against the Jew-Commie invader!

THIRD BROWNSHIRT
We're gonna wipe em all out!

> *They unfurl a large, ripped banner bearing a swastika.*

BROWNSHIRTS
Seig, Heil! Seig, Heil! Seig, Heil!

FIRST BROWNSHIRT
We're gonna have to make another one.

SECOND BROWNSHIRT
Took me a week to make that one.

THIRD BROWNSHIRT
Hey could we do, like, uh, armbands? You know like they do? You know, with the – armbands?

FIRST BROWNSHIRT
Hey. ...Listen...

JOSEPH
(has been chanting, in Yiddish) [Please God help me, please God help me, don't let them hurt me, don't let them hurt me, I'll do whatever you want me to do, I'll never run away again, not from anything you want me to face, only not this, God, I don't want them to hurt me, please God...]

SECOND BROWNSHIRT
Sounds like a–

FIRST BROWNSHIRT
Shh.

> *They creep around, looking for JOSEPH.*

Come out, come out, wherever you are.

> *They find him. He backs away. They surround him.*

SECOND BROWNSHIRT
If it talks like a Jew... and it smells like a Jew... and it looks like a Jew...

JOSEPH
No! I'm not.

FIRST BROWNSHIRT
Not what?

JOSEPH
What you say.

FIRST BROWNSHIRT
No? What are ya?

JOSEPH
I'm Christian. From Poland. "Our Father... who lives in heaven..."

FIRST BROWNSHIRT
What's your name?

JOSEPH
Pischuk. Joe Pischuk.

FIRST BROWNSHIRT
Oh yeah? Well then I guess you don't much care for Jews, do you?

JOSEPH
Jews? No. They're... bad people. Poison wells. Drink blood of little babies.

SECOND BROWNSHIRT
S'right.

JOSEPH
They're liars.

THIRD BROWNSHIRT
Yeah.

JOSEPH
Cheaters.

FIRST BROWNSHIRT
You tell it.

JOSEPH
You know what they do?

SECOND BROWNSHIRT
What, what?

JOSEPH
They take away my brother, my little brother, who I love more than all world. They say, "don't come back, or we kill him." They

don't let me see my father, not even to say goodbye. Now is five years, he is old man, maybe is dead, I don't know, I don't know.

THIRD BROWNSHIRT
Jeez. Goddamn Jews. Herb, give the kid a dollar.

SECOND BROWNSHIRT
I'm supposed to get groceries.

JOSEPH
Please, no, I–

THIRD BROWNSHIRT
Hey, hey, we gotta help each other out, right? Herb.

> *HERB hands over the money.*

Take care of yourself, kid. You ever need us, we got a clubhouse down Queen and Roncy. You'll know which it is. Let's go, boys.

BROWNSHIRTS
(exiting) Home, home for our race/Where the Jews, wops and bohunks don't play...

> *JOSEPH sits there, holding the money.*

I. xi. Train.

> *Boxcar. JOSEPH, among several men. A man sings the first verse and chorus of "No Depression in Heaven."*

> *The train doors slide open. A SOLDIER stands there.*

SOLDIER
Alright, you stiffs, you bindle stiffs, out! Out! Out! Jump down now, outta that drag, let's go, look alive, this ain't no Sally Ann and I ain't Jerusalem Slim, get out there! In line there, no talking!

RELIEF WORKER
What's the rush?

SOLDIER
No talking, I said. Get that damn smile off your face, johnny boy, this ain't no pool hall. Think you're doing with all that luggage, going on vacation? Shut your moat, keep moving! Keep moving, all a ya, what is this, the three-legged race? In line, in line, not too close, I don't want your walking dandruff. Whoa, whoa, what is this, you pack a couch, or what? Move it, move yer ass before I kick you back up your mother's hole. Alright, face front, you stiffs and get those lugs open: this is a relief camp, established

by the Canadian government to get you lazy pieces of trash off
the street, off the rails, off the dole and on your feet doing
something decent with your otherwise useless lives. What are
you looking at, bohunk? Now let's get a few things clear. You're
in the middle of nowhere, and you try to hightail it outta here,
nowhere is exactly where you're gonna get to, unless you happen
to be particularly adept at wrestling bears, which from the looks
of you ragged pieces of filth is about as likely as you sorry fucks
ever turning into real men. What's your name, handy?

MEASURES

(upper class Brit) Measures.

SOLDIER

(affecting his accent) Oh, Measures, is it? Pardon me. I do hope
you'll find the accommodations to your liking, m'lord. I say, not
too warm for you, is it? Perhaps I can find you some shade, or
a nice Indian boy to fan you.

LAY

Listen, you can't talk to us like that. We used to work for the
Prime Minister.

MEASURES

Quiet, Lay. He's not Prime Minister anymore.

SOLDIER

What's that just come outta your hole?

LAY

I said we used to work for the Prime Minister.

SOLDIER

Is that right? Which one – Sir John A. Macdonald?

LAY

King.

SOLDIER

King? Mackenzie King?

LAY

There's only one King.

SOLDIER

That's right – and here, it's me.

Shoves his club into LAY's stomach. LAY collapses.

Get away from him. Touch that piece of trash, you'll be lying
next to him. *(to JOSEPH)* You, gazooney. What's your name,
boy?

JOSEPH
Joseph.

SOLDIER
J-J-J-Joseph. They hand out last names where you come from?

JOSEPH
Taylor...

SOLDIER
What?

JOSEPH
Taylor.... Sir.

SOLDIER
"Sir." You hear that? Kid knows how to talk to a superior. *(puts an arm around JOSEPH)* You ain't a Red, are ya?

JOSEPH
No, sir.

SOLDIER
You a Jew?

JOSEPH
No, sir.

SOLDIER
Well, guess what, Taylor? You're in charge of these stiffs. First thing you can do is get that dino to his feet and march him to Bunk 12 along with the rest of these McGoof hounds. You heard me. Double time, let's go!

I. xii. A field.

A group of relief camp workers, building a road.

MEASURES
The flies are eating me alive. My hands haven't stopped bleeding for days.

FRANCIS BROWN
What are we working on anyway? A road that starts nowhere, and goes nowhere.

LAY
(to MEASURES) So the baskets are on my head because I'm walking straight – with my head up... so that's good. Walking right to King. But why are the birds eating the bread? That's what I don't get.

MEASURES
You'll drive us all mad, Lay.

LAY
It's gotta mean something, Howard.

MEASURES
Only a dream, Lay.

LAY
Yeah. And dreams are trying to tell you things. And how is it you figure we're both having the same dream?

MEASURES
They're not the same. And they don't mean a blessed thing.

LAY
Sure they do.

FRANCIS BROWN
Cheese it, here comes Corporal Punishment.

> *LAY has stopped working. The SOLDIER wanders by.*

SOLDIER
What's the problem here?

MEASURES
He's not sleeping. And the heat doesn't help.

SOLDIER
Joseph, let's have some water over here. *(to LAY)* Stand up, you. Can't sleep, huh? Maybe a more comfortable pillow?

MEASURES
Why don't you give him a break, lad?

SOLDIER
Mind your business. And who told you to stop working, lad?

MEASURES
It's this boulder. We can't possibly move it ourselves. It needs to be blasted.

SOLDIER
Use your pickaxes. If you can lift em, you deadbeats. And any man doesn't like the work is free to leave. This ain't no prison.

MEASURES
Then why do you treat us like criminals?

SOLDIER
You wanna file a complaint with the commander?

MEASURES

No thank you. I saw what happened to the last fellow that tried that.

SOLDIER

Good, Measures. I'm very impressed. Now get back to it. *(to LAY)* Now what's this about not sleeping, Lay?

LAY

It's just. I have these dreams.

SOLDIER

Dreams, is it?

LAY

That's right. Me and him both.

SOLDIER

Oh, the two of you have dreams. That's sweet.

MEASURES

You can leave me out of this.

SOLDIER

Oh no, I don't think so. I think you're in it, friend. No, I think you'd better join us, Measures. Sounds like we've got a bit of a problem here. Sounds like you and Lay here are having bad dreams. Can't have that, oh no no no, it might interfere with your work. Now, there are doctors, you know, doctors for the mind. Yeah, and we can bring in one of these doctors, if it will prove helpful to you. Tell you what, why don't you just tell me about this dream you've been having, and I'll write it up.

MEASURES

I don't think so.

SOLDIER

Oh, I do.

LAY

I'll tell you.

SOLDIER

Shut your hole, clown.

LAY

But they're the same – why can't I tell you?

SOLDIER

I don't think you've got the stomach for it. –Go on, Measures. I'll give you three seconds to start. One – two–

MEASURES
I'm working in a field.

SOLDIER
This your dream now?

MEASURES
Yes.

SOLDIER
Okay, working in a field. What kinda field?

MEASURES
A vineyard. Picking grapes. For the Prime Minister. I'm holding the Prime Minister's silver cup in my hand. I press three grapes into the cup.

SOLDIER
Three?

MEASURES
Yes. And he drinks from the cup. Now may I return to work?

SOLDIER
Well, I don't know, Measures. I don't think I quite understand it. Um. You know what? I think I need to see it. Tell ya what. Let's play it out. Yeah, yeah. That way I'll be able to get like the importance of it.

MEASURES
I'd really rather–

SOLDIER
No, no, no, Measures. Okay, gather round, everybody. We're gonna show you Measures' dream, and then we'll all help him try to figure out what it means? Okay? Okay. Now, uh, I'll be King, how's that? Look at me, I'm King. Now, you give me the uhh, cup. Joseph give him some water.

JOSEPH
Corporal–

SOLDIER
Give him some water.

JOSEPH
Corporal, I–

SOLDIER
Give him some fucking water, Joe. Alright, now you start walking to me, Measures. Bring me the cup. Alright, this is

good. Yeah, I think I'm starting to understand now. *(as KING)* Well, whattaya got there, Measures? I can't hear you.

MEASURES
A cup of wine, sir.

SOLDIER
For me?

MEASURES
Yes, sir.

SOLDIER
Well, that is very kind of you, Measures. Let me drink of the cup.

The SOLDIER drinks the water, then spits it back in MEASURES' face. The SOLDIER laughs, walks away.

Well, so much for dreams.

MEASURES raises the pickaxe, charges at the SOLDIER. JOSEPH steps in the way.

JOSEPH
Water?

MEASURES
Get out of my way.

JOSEPH
(sotto) Your dream. I understand. King will give you back your job.

SOLDIER
Out of the way, Joe.

JOSEPH
The three grapes, they are three days. King will send for you in three days. But not if you attack this man.

MEASURES puts the pick down.

SOLDIER
Remember, you're free to leave anytime. Alright, what's everybody standing around for? You think you were sent here to loaf? I gotta file a report...

The SOLDIER goes. MEASURES returns to work.

JOSEPH
When he sends for you... you will take me with you?

MEASURES
Get away from me. Do you hear?

JOSEPH
Take me with you. I have to leave this place. I haven't done anything to–

MEASURES
Leave me alone, or I'll tell that bastard where he can sniff out a real Red, and a Jew to boot. You think I don't hear your Jew prayers at night? For all I know you're casting a spell, cursing the lot of us.

JOSEPH
Take me with you. Promise me you will take me with you.

SOLDIER
(off) Joe, over here with that water!

MEASURES
Course. Just as soon as Mr. King sends for me. Now if you don't mind, I have work to do.

MEASURES returns to work.

LAY
What about me, Joe? What about my dream? There were three baskets. Just like Measures. There were three. Does that mean King's gonna send for me too? –Well, come on, tell me. Tell me!

JOSEPH
No. King will not send for you. In three days, you will be dead.

SOLDIER
Joe! Now!

JOSEPH goes.

MEASURES
Never mind that, Robert. It's a lot of nonsense. Nonsense.

I. xiii. Barracks.

The men relax after work. The SOLDIER enters.

SOLDIER
Mail call. Line up. Higgins. Lay. Frederickson. Brown. Gunnarson. Gould. Norman.

FRANCIS BROWN
Hey. Mine's been opened.

SOLDIER
Take it up with the commander. Summers. Higsby.

FRANCIS BROWN
It gets opened every time!

SOLDIER
Like I said, take it up with the commander. Measures, yours wasn't opened. It's from King.

MEASURES takes it, rips it open. The others stand around, waiting to hear what's in the letter. LAY is in bed.

FRANCIS BROWN
Well? You gonna tell us? What's the old bugger gotta say?

MEASURES
Says... sweet Jesus... he's taking me back.

FRANCIS BROWN
What about Lay? Does it say anything about Lay?

MEASURES
No.

Everyone turns to look at LAY. The SOLDIER goes to him.

SOLDIER
Lay. Lay.

JOSEPH
(to MEASURES) Remember what I said.

MEASURES
Lay? ...Lay... Lay!

I. xiv. Kingsmere, estate of William Lyon Mackenzie King, the Once and Future Prime Minister of Canada. Summer, 1932.

A path leading into a forest. A bench. KING and JOSEPH.

JOSEPH
Is very beautiful here.

KING
Ah. It speaks. You know who I am.

JOSEPH
You are Prime Minister.

KING
Was Prime Minister. I hope to be so again one day, much to the dismay of certain members of my Party. It's Joseph, isn't it?

JOSEPH

Yes. Sorry for not speaking more, I – my English – is not so very good.

KING

Better than some. At least you have manners, the sign of a boy who's been properly raised. Where are you from?

JOSEPH

Poland.

KING

Where, exactly?

JOSEPH

You wouldn't know it.

KING

I may have to revise my assessment of your upbringing. Have you a family?

JOSEPH

No.

KING

In Poland, I mean.

JOSEPH

I have no family.

KING

It's all very presumptuous of me, isn't it? My apologies. Well, that will be all.

JOSEPH

All?

KING

Yes. You may return to work.

JOSEPH

But Measures, he...

KING

Yes?

JOSEPH

Said you wanted to see me.

KING

Yes, I did. Wanted to get to know you a little bit. But you don't seem to want to tell me anything about yourself. And I'm certainly not going to force you. Good day. Good day.

Pause.

JOSEPH

I was born in Luzniki. Shtetl. My father is a tailor, my mother died when I was five. She died giving birth to my brother. I have many brothers, they sent me away. They sent me away, because they hate me. They send me to this country, because they hate me. Can you understand this? What did I do to make them hate me? Since I come, all hate me. I work, I work hard, and all time people hate. Since I am small child, my father say, "Joseph, be good, and study, God will look after you, you are special child." Look at me, Mr. King. This is how God looks after his special children? Yes? Okay. I do it. Because my father wants me to. I don't make trouble, but always I get into it. I tell you more? I work in factory, Toronto. Terrible, but I need money, so I work, work hard. So hard, I am treated better than others. And the men hate me for this. One day, boss comes to me, says, "Communists taking over shop, tell me names, is Depression, shop will close if you don't help me fight them, pray with me! Pray with me to defeat them!" "No," I say. "No, and no and no." But he don't listen. Okay? So I have no job; I sleep in park; I eat from garbage cans; one day, man comes to me in street, says "I have job for you. Is far away, but is job." I get on train, train goes long, long, long. Takes me to camp. A kind of prison. I am put in charge of men in barracks. So again I am hated. Okay? Now I have told you all. Now I don't speak. I go to work on your path.

KING

You didn't tell me everything, though, did you, Joseph?

JOSEPH

What more you want to know?

KING

Check your anger, young man. I won't stand for it. You've had a rough time of it. I'm sorry for that. But that chip on your shoulder will get you nowhere.

MEASURES returns with drinks.

Wonderful. Joseph, you simply must try this lemonade. Measures makes it himself. Measures, give Joseph a glass. But there I go being presumptuous again. Would you care for some lemonade? Ah, but you're not talking. *(drinks)* Oh, that's marvelous. *(smacks his lips)* No need for a breeze when–

JOSEPH
I will have. Please.

MEASURES pours. JOSEPH drinks.

KING
Do you know I wrote a paper condemning sweatshop practices, and that was more than thirty years ago, my boy. More than thirty years. So you don't need to tell me about improving conditions. I know all about that. Yes, I do. *(seeing JOSEPH drink)* Good, isn't it? I'm all for improving conditions. I'm afraid we're behind the times in the country in a number of – is there something you need, Measures?

MEASURES
No, sir. Will that be all?

KING
Apparently.

MEASURES goes.

Joseph. Tell me about this ability of yours. This power. Come, Joseph, you know what I'm talking about. You interpret dreams. You did it for my men. Mind you, Lay was not a healthy man. You could have seen that. Just as you might well have guessed that Measures would win his job back. He need only have let you know that he was fired for an offense he did not commit. Then it would simply have been a matter of adding two and two. The thing that grabbed my attention, was that you had it down to the very day. You saw the future. Predicted it.

JOSEPH
It was shown to me.

KING
God showed it to you.

JOSEPH
Yes.

KING
Has he shown you other dreams? Dreams about the future?

JOSEPH
No.

KING
How long have you had this ability? –Come, Joseph.

JOSEPH
Long time.

KING

Years?

JOSEPH

Since I am child. The night before my brother was born, I dream our mother would die giving birth to him. She died.

KING

Did you tell anyone about this dream?

JOSEPH

My father. He said, "Never speak of these things." Is only time in my life he is angry with me.

KING

Was angry. My own father was a kind man, too.

JOSEPH

Excuse me, Mr. King. My father was not kind. Except to me.

Pause.

KING

Joseph, I too have been having dreams of late, disturbing dreams. I have tried all manner of interpretation for them, but have received no satisfactory answer. Perhaps you can give me one.

JOSEPH

Please.

MEASURES returns, holding a tray.

KING

Yes, what is it, Measures?

MEASURES

I thought you and the boy might like something to eat, sir.

KING

Very thoughtful of you, Measures. Put it down.

MEASURES

Very good, sir. Only it's turned to dust. Everything. There's nothing to eat, sir. We've had to burn the wheat, and the sheep, and the corn. But there are still fourteen head of cattle; seven healthy, seven sickly. I've asked the lads to put down the healthy ones, sir.

KING

What on earth for?

MEASURES

How else shall we feed the sickly ones? Come, see for yourself.

A series of rifle shots. KING looks off.

You see how the sickly ones devour the healthy? Yet it's having no effect whatsoever. The sickly cows are as emaciated as they were before. What shall we do, sir?

FRANCIS returns.

FRANCIS

Prime Minister... Prime Minister, sir.

KING

What is it, Francis?

FRANCIS

Sir, the trees... we spent all morning bringing down a stand of pines, all withered and mangled, seven in all. Only, as soon as we felled em, there was a great wind, from the east; we had to hide our eyes; when we opened em again, the mightiest oak you ever did see stood in place of the ones we'd just brought down! So we got to knockin' down that one, sir; only the very moment it toppled over, another shot up. So we set on that one, and yet another one grew; six times in all, now comes the seventh. The lads don't mind. Happy for the work, they are. Shall we keep at it, sir?

FRANCIS goes back into the forest. MEASURES has gone.

KING

What do you make of it, Joseph?

JOSEPH

God has shown what is going to happen. There will be a famine.

KING

Where?

JOSEPH

In your land.

KING

In Canada? But if anything, we have an *abundance* of food.

JOSEPH

The wheat will not grow. The rain will not fall. Seven years it will last – this is the meaning of the burnt harvest, and the sickly cattle.

KING

And after these seven years?

JOSEPH

All will change.

KING
>Change how?

JOSEPH
>For better. This is the vision of the trees. Men go back to
>work. Factories open again. Much activity. Preparations...
>preparations...

KING
>For what?

JOSEPH
>A great... a great event...

KING
>To do with my country?

JOSEPH
>Yes. You are in charge. People look to you, to make decisions.

KING
>In seven years, you say? 1939. You say I'll be Prime Minister
>then?

JOSEPH
>This is in the interpretation.

>>*KING rises. JOSEPH moves as though to help.*

KING
>No no. I can still walk. *(calls out)* Measures! *(to JOSEPH)* It's this
>arthritis. Makes it difficult to sleep. You see the path, where it
>ends? It's going to continue on, another fifty yards. To the guest
>cottage. It's something of a nuisance, you see, for visitors,
>because they have to take the long way around. I wasn't sure
>I ought to be taking down the trees, you know.

>>*MEASURES enters.*

KING
>Measures, the guest cottage, does it have clean bedding?

MEASURES
>I believe so, sir. Are we expecting company, sir?

KING
>It's for Mr. Taylor.

MEASURES
>In the guest cottage, sir?

KING
>Yes, Measures, and I'll thank you to watch your tone.

MEASURES
> Yes, of course. Is it a permanent move, sir?

KING
> Best ask Mr. Taylor. Oh, and Measures. Have the car brought round in an hour. We'll be going into town. Get Mr. Taylor some new clothes.

MEASURES
> Will Mr. Taylor be dining with you, Mr. King? –Very good, sir.

> *MEASURES goes.*

KING
> I can't tell you how many servants I've gone through in the last few years. Measures is a decent sort. Good worker, but every once in a while he tries to show me up in that British way which I simply can't – what is it, Joseph? Joseph?

JOSEPH
> No. Is nothing you can help me with. Mr. King, please don't do this.

KING
> Don't do what, Joseph?

JOSEPH
> Treat me well. I don't want them to hate me.

KING
> Joseph, a man believes the world to be of spirit or of matter, one or the other, and from a very young age. I think you know where I stand, and, if you don't mind my saying so, I think I know where you do. Or do you think it's a coincidence that you were brought here? I tell you, there's no such thing as coincidence. There is only destiny. Mine is to lead this country. As for you – you are on a path. God has put you on it. You have no choice. Let me show you where you'll be staying. This way, through the forest.

> *They go into the forest.*

— • — Act II — • —

II. i. Kingsmere. The path. October, 1935.

MEASURES, FRANCIS, JACK, conducting a seance. JOSEPH watching.

FRANCIS
Oh, spirits of the dead, we the servants at Kingsmere wish to know what is to be our fate, now that King has won the election and is to return to Ottawa. Not that we mind the latter part, spirits, but we do desire to know if we are to be retained.

Pause. FRANCIS tilts his head back.

"Servants of Kingsmere... know this... you mean less to King than his little dog. One of you is to be fired this very night."

JACK
Who, spirit, who?

FRANCIS
"It is not determined."

JACK
Who are you, spirit?

FRANCIS
"I am he what used to walk these grounds."

JACK
A long time ago, spirit?

FRANCIS
"Not so long. Now I walk these grounds again. I want vengeance for ill-treatment and death. I am Robert Lay! Mwa-ha-ha-ha!"

MEASURES breaks from the group.

MEASURES
That's not funny! That's not at all funny!

FRANCIS
(laughing) Aw, come on, Howard, I's only playing.

MEASURES looks into the forest.

JOSEPH
Bit of a low one, Francis.

JACK
(nodding towards MEASURES) You know he sees him.

JOSEPH
There's nothing out there, Howard.

JACK
Hang on. It's my turn. Come on, your hands.

MEASURES
Leave me out of this.

JACK
What about you, Joe?

JOSEPH
I'm for bed.

JACK
Oh, yeah? Whose?

FRANCIS
Lay off, Jack, we're celebrating.

JACK
Tomorrow morning, this one goes to Ottawa, don't he? While
the rest of us keep slaving away here. So the question is, how
does a boy like this rise so quickly through the ranks? How is it
he gets plucked from the mud, cleaned up, sent to university,
come back all spic-and-span, talking like a real regular Canadian
boy.

JOSEPH
Well Jack, he was going to send you – but you're so good at
cleaning his toilet.

JACK stands.

FRANCIS
Come on, Jack, all's fair in love and hate.

JACK
Watch your step. Does the old man even know you're a Jew?
We all know what he thinks of your kind. Only reason he bought
that cottage was cause he didn't want kikes for neighbours.
I wonder what he'd make of it. I know. The spirits will tell me.
Your hands, Francis. Quickly, I feel the spirits upon me. *(joins
hands with FRANCIS, tilts back his head)* "It is I, Mrs. King, the
mother of the once and future Prime Minister. There is one
among you who will be found out this evening for what he truly
is. If he don't watch his step."

KING has entered. He carries a gift.

MEASURES
Straighten up.

FRANCIS
Oh, allo Mr. King. Or should I say Prime Minister?

JACK
Yeah, congratulations, Mih uh Prime Minister. Great victory. Three cheers for the Prime Minister. Hip hip–

JACK & FRANCIS
Hooray!

JACK
Hip hip–

KING
That's enough.

MEASURES
Very sorry, sir. The boys only wanted to celebrate the victory, sir.

Pause.

KING
I heard a noise. In the shed.

MEASURES
In the shed, sir? What sort of noise?

FRANCIS
Bloody porkypine, sir. Come on, Jack, we'll take its bloody head off.

KING
You, too, Measures.

MEASURES
Me, sir?

KING
Howard, what's gotten into you? You've become clumsy and forgetful.

MEASURES
I'm fine, sir. Come along, then, lads.

KING and JOSEPH are left alone.

JOSEPH
I'm sorry about this, sir. I came out with the intention of asking them to... keep their voices down. Instead–

KING
Quite alright, Joseph. No need to explain yourself.

JOSEPH

Is there something–?

KING

Mm?

JOSEPH

You told me you were going to turn in early, sir.

KING

Yes. Just my leg. The damp gets right inside it, you know.

JOSEPH

Perhaps the doctor could–

KING

The doctor, the doctor. I'm old, that's all.

JOSEPH

You're not.

KING

Yes, yes – and don't try flattery on me, young man, I've been a politician longer than you've been alive. Anyway, it doesn't become you.

JOSEPH

Have I done something? To upset you?

KING

I should say you have. You interpreted my dreams, you predicted the future, and it's scaring the daylights out of me, young man, it really is. For years I—decades—I listened to spirits. I heard the voices of my mother, my grandfather, felt their presence. I would ask them, "Pray, tell me, how will such-and-such turn out? What course of action should I take?" A man needs diversions, you see, and when a man doesn't marry, he needs them all the more. Something to while away the hours while he's trying to forget that he's whiling away alone. You see, it didn't matter, Joseph. Some part of me understood that it was a parlour game. But then you came along, you said such-and-such would happen— and not only what but when—and here it is three years later, and every such-and-such has come to pass. The drought, crop failures, locusts, too – at just the moment you said it would and I'm perfectly fearful, my lad, I'm petrified, I'm beyond, oh Lord, this really goes against it, you know this really goes against everything I–

Pause.

I have to tell you, young man, and you really should know this. I was sure those visions were telling me that I ought to step down. Yes, and I fully expected you to confirm that, because Measures had explained to me all that you had done. Then you said what you said, and I was afraid, because I knew you were right, that I was meant to stay on, and see the country through what is to come. Only what if I'm not up to the task?

JOSEPH

Prime Minister, you too were put on a path.

KING

It's a fearful thing to be told the future. It must be more fearful still to be able to see it. Joseph, a gift such as yours, in the wrong hands, could be used to foresee anything, anything at all – from the outcome of a horse race, to the rise and fall of stocks, to the likelihood of war.

JOSEPH

Prime Minister. If God, in his infinite wisdom, should choose to send you a vision of a horse race, then God, in his infinite wisdom, will permit me to interpret it for you.

KING

(laughing) You've cheered me, my boy. *(presents the gift)* Come, open it.

    JOSEPH opens the present; a silver cup.

JOSEPH

I can't accept this.

KING

You can, and you will, a sign of our bond. *(taps him on the cheek; he lets his hand linger on JOSEPH's face, then takes it away)* There's much to do. Preparations. Preparations. You can start by telling Jack to pack his things.

    MEASURES returns.

Howard? What was it? What's the matter, man?

MEASURES

Prime Minister... I wish to inform you that... I must leave this place, and seek employment elsewhere. Immediately.

KING

Howard...

MEASURES

They say everything happens for a reason, sir. I only wish I knew what it was.

II. ii. Ottawa. The Prime Minister's Office. 1936.

*KING, JOSEPH and Frederick BLAIR, head of the Immigration
Branch.*

BLAIR
...with the express purpose of fomenting rebellion.

JOSEPH
They don't seem to have made much headway.

BLAIR
I beg your pardon?

JOSEPH
Frankly, sir, the only reason these people need to "force open"
the doors is that the doors have been so tightly shut against
them these last few years.

BLAIR
The reason those doors have been shut, young man, is to prevent
our way of life from being undermined.

JOSEPH
Oh, I don't know sir. Our way of life could use a good
undermining now and again.

BLAIR
Prime Minister–

JOSEPH
The Prime Minister's own grandfather led a rebellion against this
country's former overlords.

KING
Let's keep my grandfather out of this, shall we? –But proceed.

JOSEPH
Mr. Blair, do you know what it is to leave your home? To watch
it disappear, and then find yourself in another land, strange and
unaccommodating, seeking one small show of kindness?

KING
Sounds rather like Parliament.

BLAIR
Young man, I need no lecture on the tribulations of the
immigrant; I was brought here myself as a child, and learned
to make my way in life without pity – and glad I am for it.
A nation that allows its immigration policy to be hijacked by
sentiment–

JOSEPH
> Hijacked!

BLAIR
> —And not—yes, hijacked—rather than ruled by reason is a very weak nation indeed, and doomed to fail. But I speak only as Head of the Immigration Branch, and not as the Prime Minister's most trusted adviser, who no doubt will advise the Prime Minister that we accept these people and their stories with nary a thought for the consequences.

JOSEPH
> The consequences for whom?

BLAIR
> For the Canadian people, young buck, who have made it clear that they will not accept these refugees, with their dark and secretive ways. Quebec is especially virulent in its opposition; will the Prime Minister risk the very unity of the country for the sake of a handful of undesirables?

JOSEPH
> I don't see how you can call 700 people who've made their way–

KING
> Alright. Alright.

> *Pause.*

> They have no entry visas for Canada?

BLAIR
> No, Prime Minister.

KING
> But in theory they could apply for them.

BLAIR
> In theory.

KING
> But not from here.

BLAIR
> No, sir. They would have to apply from their homelands.

KING
> Well, there it is. We'll tell them—it's quite simple—they're not being denied entry, they're simply being asked to go through the usual channels to um – you follow?

BLAIR
> I do.

KING
Their applications will be assessed fairly, without prejudice.

BLAIR
Of course.

KING
We'll send a delegation to speak with them. A photo wouldn't hurt. Make sure the *Star*'s on hand, the *Globe*, the *Free Press* – the Quebec papers, *Le Devoyer*.

BLAIR
I'll arrange it.

KING
I'd like someone from my office to be involved.

BLAIR
Sir?

KING
Joseph. Joseph?

JOSEPH
Prime Minister.

KING
You'll go. As my emissary.

BLAIR
Prime Minister, if I may. This is a very delicate matter, requiring great sensitivity.

KING
I couldn't agree with you more there, Freddy. You see, and that's why I've chosen Joseph; he's from that part of the world. He knows these people. Speaks their language.

BLAIR
Does he?

KING
Oh, Russian, Polish—he's fluent, completely—only you wouldn't guess, would you?

BLAIR
It never occurred to me, I must admit.

KING
Then it's settled. Now we really must move on. Oh, Freddy – I've been meaning to ask. I'm having terrible luck with the servants lately at Kingsmere. My butler Measures has decided to return

to England, and there's gratitude for you. Any chance you might have some domestics coming in?

BLAIR

I could easily find a Scandinavian or two if you like.

KING

Scandinavians? They tend to cook rather rich foods, don't they? Creamy.

BLAIR

I'm sure they'll cook whatever you desire, Prime Minister.

KING

Well, I'll leave it with you. Good day.

BLAIR

Prime Minister.

BLAIR goes.

JOSEPH

Did you catch that? "Young buck."

KING

Yes, well, that was a bit of dirty pool on your part, wasn't it, raising the spectre of my grandfather? Don't get me wrong; it was a good shot. Only mind you're not too clever with Freddy Blair.

JOSEPH

If it's ever my misfortune to meet him again, I'll throw myself at his feet.

KING

You may want to be wearing a helmet. In any case you're going to have to learn to work with him.

JOSEPH

Why?

KING

Because, "young buck," you're going to be my point man on this. And I don't just mean this business with the ship; it's the refugee issue altogether. It's only going to get worse, and I need to keep on top of it – without seeming to. And don't tell me you're not the right man for the job. You're already my eyes – now you'll be my ears, as well. Only don't let it get to your head. You know how power corrupts.

JOSEPH

Absolutely.

II. iii. Halifax. Immigration Centre.

> *JUDAH, REUBEN and SIMON, in shadow. JOSEPH enters, with the guard.*

GUARD
They're in here, Mr. Taylor. *(offers a handkerchief)* You might want this, sir. There's a report that some of the passengers are ill. And the smell you know?

JOSEPH
It's so dark in here. Couldn't they be in a room with windows?

GUARD
Orders from Mr. Blair, sir.

JOSEPH
Do any of them speak English?

GUARD
Apparently they held a vote to see who'd speak for the group. All I can tell you is there was a lot of shouting. These folks won.

JOSEPH
Let's begin. Step forward there.

> *JUDAH, REUBEN and SIMON emerge. JOSEPH reflexively steps back. Covers his face with the handkerchief.*

JUDAH
This is the man we are speaking to?

GUARD
Yeah, just hold on there. You alright, Mr. Taylor?

JOSEPH
Just – the heat. There's no air in here. Have you got the passenger manifest?

GUARD
Yes, sir.

JOSEPH
Tell them to wait a minute.

> *JOSEPH looks through the manifest. Finds his brothers' names. Tries to compose himself. Turns back.*

Alright. *(to the GUARD)* Tell them not to come too close.

GUARD
That's far enough.

l to r: Dmitry Chepovetsky, Kyle Horton, Alex Poch-Goldin.
photo by Cylla von Tiedemann

JUDAH

Sir, my name is Judah Dubczanski. I am with my brothers. There are ten of us all together, plus wives and children on ship. Is very bad now in Poland since Pilsudski died.

SIMON

[Forget the history lesson, ask him if they're gonna take us.]

REUBEN

[They won't, they won't, and you know why.]

JUDAH

Please, excuse. They are anxious. You see, Pilsudski, he protect Jews, and now he is dead, so we're afraid Poles will start again with pogroms. We have papers. We have visas. Our Uncle, he has jobs for us, in New York, ship was supposed to go to New York but instead – look, here are papers... will you look?

JOSEPH

(to the GUARD) Hand me the passports.

> *GUARD takes the passports from JUDAH, hands them to JOSEPH, who walks away.*

REUBEN

[You know why this is happening, don't you? We're being punished. Because of what we did to Joseph.]

JUDAH

[If you believe that, you're a fool. Or more religious than you let on.]

SIMON

[He's become both lately.]

REUBEN

[I said not to harm him, didn't I? I said, "We'll just talk to him, put a scare into him," but no, no, you had to have your way, because you're filled with hate.]

JUDAH

[Step away from me.]

REUBEN

[You've never believed in anything, Judah. You gave up on the Bund, you'll give up on your own family.]

SIMON

[You'd better shut up now. You're not running things anymore.]

> *JOSEPH walks back to JUDAH.*

JOSEPH
You say there are ten of you?

JUDAH
Yes.

JOSEPH
All brothers?

JUDAH
Yes.

JOSEPH
Are there more?

JUDAH
One.

JOSEPH
Where is he?

JUDAH
At home.

JOSEPH
Why didn't he come with you?

JUDAH
He couldn't.

JOSEPH
Why?

JUDAH
Our father would not let him go.

JOSEPH
He's still alive? –He must be a very old man, to have had so many children.

JUDAH
He is.

>   *Pause.*

JOSEPH
Who paid your passage?

JUDAH
Our father.

JOSEPH
It's a lot of money.

JUDAH
Our father is a very wealthy man.

JOSEPH
What do you mean by that?

JUDAH
Only to say, he has money.

>*Pause.*

JOSEPH
You think I don't know who you are? –You're spies.

JUDAH
Spies?

JOSEPH
Communist spies. Trying to bribe me.

JUDAH
No, this is–

JOSEPH
Don't you speak to me!

>*Silence.*

We have had a number of young men from Eastern Europe come to our country, pretending to be farmers, only to infiltrate our cities and towns to sow dissension. This story of yours – ten brothers, all travelling together, and another one at home...

REUBEN
[What's he talking about?]

JUDAH
[He says we're spies.]

REUBEN
[Spies?]

JUDAH
Mister, we are tailors. Look at our passports, our visas.

JOSEPH
These could be forgeries.

JUDAH
No. Please. Look, I show you something, okay?

JOSEPH
Well.

JUDAH

Is picture. *(He takes a picture from his jacket pocket.)* Of our family. Was taken many years ago. My brothers, there, you see, and our father.

> *JOSEPH looks at the photo.*

JOSEPH

There are twelve here. You said there were ten and one more at home.

JUDAH

One died. Him. Was killed.

JOSEPH

You must miss him very much.

> *Pause.*

How was he killed?

JUDAH

Was kidnapped. Murdered.

JOSEPH

Must have been very difficult for your father, to lose a son, and in so brutal a fashion.

> *JUDAH looks to REUBEN and SIMON.*

Why did you look to your brothers just now?

JUDAH

Your questions. I don't understand.

JOSEPH

They're simple enough. Did your father seek justice for his son's murder?

JUDAH

They were never caught, the men who did this.

JOSEPH

Ah, no?

JUDAH

This is how it is in my world. Has always been this way. Always will be this way. So we come here. Will you let us in?

> *Pause.*

JOSEPH

You'll have to go back. And reapply, as a complete family unit.

JUDAH
Complete?

JOSEPH
With your father and your younger brother.

JUDAH
Is not possible. Our father is not well, please, mister, he would not survive, he is old, going blind.

JOSEPH
Blind?

JUDAH
He sees only little.

JOSEPH
And your brother?

JUDAH
Our father will not let him go. He loves him more than all others.

JOSEPH
Then you'll have to convince him. Or none of you will be admitted.

JUDAH
We don't even want to come to this country. We want to go to United States.

JOSEPH
Well, fate seems to have brought you here. It's having a good laugh at your expense.

JUDAH
[He says fate is laughing at us.]

REUBEN
[You see? You see? Punishment.]

SIMON
[Shut your goddamn mouth!]

JUDAH
Mister, you are smart man, yes? You know what is happening all over Europe? You are going to send us back to that?

JOSEPH
You think you're the only ones who suffer?

>   *JOSEPH walks among them.*

Name?

JUDAH
He is Reuben.

JOSEPH
Reuben. I don't think I can trust this one.

He goes to SIMON.

JUDAH
Simon.

SIMON
[What? Why's he looking at me?]

JOSEPH
Yes – he'll do.

JUDAH
What you are going to do with him?

JOSEPH
I'm going to keep him. If you're spies, you'll leave him behind. If you're brothers, truly brothers, you'll come back for him. Won't you.

SIMON
[What's going on?]

JUDAH explains to SIMON, as:

JOSEPH
(to the GUARD) Escort these men back to the ship. Except for that one; he's coming with me. Make sure the others are given food, medical supplies – whatever they need.

GUARD
Yes, Mr. Taylor.

SIMON
[What? No! Why?]

GUARD
This way, please. This way.

The GUARD leads the brothers away.

SIMON
[Reuben? Judah?]

II. iv. Kingsmere. Servants quarters.

JOSEPH and SIMON.

JOSEPH
This is your room. Room. Walls. Bed. You don't understand a
word I'm saying, do you? Dumb as an ox. I'd like to put your eyes
out, do you know that? I'm not going to make it easy for you.
I could speak your language, but that might give me away. I was
a boy when you sent me here; seventeen. I'm 28 now, a man.

Pause.

We never had much to say anyway. Window. Curtain. Floor.
I need to know things. Eleven years that you took from me, and
you're going to tell me every detail. Who was born, and who has
died; who married, and how many children. And how is Father.
Let's try this. Button. There's something your pea-brain can
grasp. Button. Hole. Hole. Like the one you hoped I'd
disappeared into.

FRANCIS walks in.

FRANCIS
Oh, didn't mean to uhh–

JOSEPH
It's fine, Francis. This is the new man. He's replacing Jack.

FRANCIS
What is he, then?

JOSEPH
He's Polish, if that's what you mean.

FRANCIS
I didn't mean nothing by it, sir. Does he speak English?

JOSEPH
You'll have to teach it to him.

FRANCIS
Bloody hell, I barely speak it myself, sir.

JOSEPH
Show him the grounds tomorrow. Point out simple things. Rock.
Tree. Dog. Try that a few thousand times, see if he catches on.
And try to make it clear to him that there's nowhere for him to
run to.

FRANCIS
How shall I do that, sir?

JOSEPH

Use your imagination, Francis. I'll leave you to it, then.

JOSEPH goes.

FRANCIS

Right, sir. What's his name, then? –Well. Good a place to start as any. I – I, me – me, I – am – Francis. My name – name – is – Francis. Fraaaaaawwwwwn sssssis. Frawn ciss.

Pause.

Is my name. How you doin? –Right.

Finds a bottle of booze. Holds it up.

Nothing like greasing the wheels to get the old machinery going, eh?

II. v. Luzniki. Dubczanski home.

JACOB, near blindness. With BENJAMIN. Three weeks later.

JACOB

Just my luck to be left with the one who doesn't speak. You can't read to me from the Torah. You can't sing to me. Even Pischuk doesn't come around any more. The man was an idiot, he had nothing to say, but he could at least talk about the weather. Conversation, Benjamin, it's the last thing that's left to me, and I'm to be denied even that. So we are punished for our sins.

REUBEN and JUDAH enter.

JACOB

Who is it? Who's there? Why don't they speak? ...It's them. They didn't make it. They didn't get through. Say something.

JUDAH

We made it.

REUBEN

They sent us back.

JACOB

Why? What did you do?

JUDAH

We did nothing. Uncle Sol screwed up. We never had quota numbers. The Americans wouldn't take us. We ended up in Canada. They wouldn't take us, either.

JACOB
Why not? Did you say something to make them angry?

REUBEN
Judah did the talking.

JACOB
That's why I ask.

JUDAH
I said nothing. They sent a man to speak to us, he treated us like filth.

JACOB
What man?

JUDAH
I don't know, some man, some little nothing of a man.

JACOB
You probably said something to upset him. Always letting your pride get in the way. I tried to teach you, to show you, every once in a while try ingratiating yourself–

JUDAH
I did nothing!

JACOB
Don't you raise your voice to me.

REUBEN
It's true, Father. This man, he–. Judah showed him our papers, pleaded with him, he wouldn't listen.

JACOB
Like gets like.

> *Beat.*

Is everyone safe? ...Well?

JUDAH
He kept Simon.

JACOB
"Kept?" How "kept?"

JUDAH
Accused him of being a spy, a Communist. Accused us all.

JACOB
This is your doing; you see what you've brought on us? God, God, God, have I lost another son?

REUBEN
No. He's to be taken good care of, and returned to us, on condition we show this man that we're not spies, but truly brothers, a family.

JACOB
You showed him your papers.

JUDAH
He wants to see Benjamin, and you.

JACOB
No.

JUDAH
He–

JACOB
This is my home. I'm not going anywhere. And I won't let you take Benjamin. No, no, Benjamin, come to me, Benjamin!

JUDAH removes a bundle of money from his suitcase.

JUDAH
We found money... in our bags... hundreds... thousands...

JACOB
How? Did you steal it?

JUDAH
I found it in my trunk.

REUBEN opens his suitcase.

REUBEN
And in mine: tickets. Steamship tickets. Enough for all of us. He must have done this; that man.

JACOB
It's a trap.

REUBEN
Father–

JACOB
He wants you to bring Benjamin, and when you get there, he'll arrest the bunch of you, and I'll lose you all.

JUDAH
You'll only lose us if we stay.

REUBEN
Father, please. Already, in one month, things have gotten worse. We could see it ourselves, as soon as we stepped off the ship. We have a chance, let us take it.

JUDAH

If you won't go, let us have Benjamin. We'll protect him.

JACOB

Protect him? Did you protect Joseph? Now, no more. You're all against me. Everything is against me.

Pause.

We'll be safe here. This madness will pass. It will pass.

II. vi. Kingsmere. Joseph's bedroom. November, 1938.

JOSEPH, in bed. Very dark. A single light shines from above. His brothers file in. He rises from bed, goes among them.

JOSEPH

Reuben... Asher... Daniel... Judah... are you all here? But how did you get here? And Father, is he well?

No one answers. BENJAMIN is crying.

Benjamin, what is it?

BENJAMIN continues to cry.

Benjamin, it's alright, I'm here... I'm here...

BENJAMIN points up to the light. They are all looking at the light. The light disappears. SIMON approaches JOSEPH, who is asleep; covers JOSEPH's mouth. JOSEPH wakes.

SIMON

Quiet. Say nothing. Understand?

SIMON takes his hand away. He holds a newspaper.

Read.

Throws the paper at him. JOSEPH looks at it.

[It started last night. Germany, Austria. Windows smashed, synagogues on fire. Fifty took their own lives. I know you can understand me. This is what you sent them back to. And don't say, "but this is Germany, but this is Austria." Don't tell me, "These things won't happen in Poland." I've seen such things, and worse, much worse. You sent them back. You sent my brothers back. Two years, two years and not a word. I don't even know if they're alive. My wife. My children, and Father. No one writes me. Or do they? Do they?]

JOSEPH, still.

(with accent) Send... me... back.

    JOSEPH, shakes his head no.

Send me back. *(weeping)* Send me back. Send me back.

    FRANCIS comes in.

FRANCIS
Everything alright, sir?

JOSEPH
Yes, fine. He's had some unhappy news.

FRANCIS
I see, sir. Yeah, getting nasty over there, isn't it? Funny you didn't see it coming.

JOSEPH
Good night, Francis.

FRANCIS
Night, sir.

    FRANCIS goes.

JOSEPH
[They've been in Luzniki these last two years.]

SIMON
[You speak Polish?]

JOSEPH
[They're fine. *(retrieves letters)* None of this has touched them. But your father, he won't part with your youngest brother.]

SIMON
[Why are you doing this to me? You know we're not what you say. All those stories you made me tell you – you think I could make that up? You think I could invent a family like that? You know we're brothers.]

JOSEPH
[That I don't know; that I need to see.]

SIMON
[If they don't come back, if a single one of them is hurt, I will come for you.]

JOSEPH
[Now you're sounding like a brother. Go on and read your letters. Read. Read.]

    SIMON starts poring through the letters.

II. vii. St Andrew's Church, Ottawa. August 1939.

The congregation sings "Forward Through the Ages." JOSEPH reads a note he's just been handed. He makes his way to KING, but is stopped.

MAX
Mr. Taylor. Mr. Taylor. Communist.

JOSEPH
Max...?

MAX
(going to JOSEPH) You wouldn't return my calls, so I figured I'd better come see you. Hope you don't mind. Actually, I don't care if you mind. You've developed very Catholic tastes.

JOSEPH
Presbyterian actually. The Prime Minister is a devout Christian.

MAX
And therefore so are you?

JOSEPH
My life was at stake. I promised God to do what was necessary.

MAX
Turning against your own people, was that necessary?

JOSEPH
I won't be judged.

MAX
Not down here. You really seem to have fit in, Joseph. When I saw you at first, I had to ask myself, "is this the Joseph I knew?" Maybe you ask yourself the same question. Or maybe not.

JOSEPH
Look, if you came all the way to Ottawa to take shots at me–

MAX
(looking at KING) That your boss?

JOSEPH
Walk with me.

They walk away, into the vestibule.

MAX
Pottinger's dead. Killed himself.

JOSEPH
Yes, I heard.

MAX

But did you hear how? His sons came home, found him in the shower; he'd hung himself – with a tallis. Turns out he was a Jew.

JOSEPH

I'm sorry for him.

MAX

So were the seven people who showed up to his funeral. His sons were so sorry they sold us the factory; yeah, the workers own it. Ain't that a kick?

JOSEPH

Congratulations. You bought the Promised Land.

MAX

It's not everything it was cracked up to be. But things are picking up. Thanks to your friends, the fascists, the war machine's sending money into all corners of the economy. The Canadian army wants us to make its uniforms. Thankfully, they didn't ask us to put our hearts on our sleeves.

JOSEPH

What do you mean, my "friends?"

MAX

Well, King's pals with Hitler; you're pals with King. Zip zip zip, you're a friend of the fascists.

JOSEPH

You always did talk too much.

MAX

And you not enough.

JOSEPH

How could I, with you around?

MAX

If I didn't talk so much, you wouldn't be in this fucking country. *(pause)* I need your help. I have family in Lvov. The Novgorodniks, remember? Desperate to leave. They tried America, but couldn't get quota numbers. They tried—will you listen?—They want to come here. They hear all kinds of things, all kinds of excuses why they can't come. It's all a code – you know as well as I do why they can't come. But no one says it. Instead they make up rules, so many rules, you can't believe— you have to have this much money, you must be able to work on a farm, you have to come as a family, even if your family is not all together—and they make you wait. They make you wait so long that the rules change again and you have to wait some more.

The hymn ends. "Amens." Bells.

Joseph – you can speak to the Prime Minister – listen – there is a way to get around all these stupid rules and all the waiting – it's called an Order-in-Council – it's like a decree. King can do this. You can get King to do this.

MAX tries to stuff a wad of bills into JOSEPH's pocket. JOSEPH pushes MAX's hand away.

JOSEPH
Keep your money. I'll mention it to him.

MAX
"Mention it?" You better do more than "mention" it.

JOSEPH
Or what, Max?

MAX
Or nothing – Mr. Dubczanski.

KING enters.

KING
Joseph? Joseph. Who was that you were speaking with just now?

JOSEPH
No one, sir. The fellow thought he recognised me.... The thing is, I've just received word, Germany has invaded Poland. The British Ambassador is waiting for you...

They go.

II. viii. Dubczanski home. 1941.

The sabbath. JACOB, JUDAH, REUBEN, BENJAMIN. As they eat:

JACOB
You have the money?

JUDAH
Yes, Father.

JACOB
It's twice what he gave you?

JUDAH
Yes, twice.

JACOB
And the present?

JUDAH
It's all packed.

JACOB
You'll write to Simon when you cross the border, you'll include a letter to this man, to explain to him why–

JUDAH
Father, everything's ready.

Pause.

JACOB
It's too quiet outside. Why is it so quiet? *(beat)* Make sure you stay off the main roads. And don't go in the direction of Lvov. They say the whole town's been cleared of Jews. There's not one left. Not one. Gypsies, too. Communists. Well. Stay off the main roads.... Reuben, are you eating?

REUBEN
(not eating) Yes, Father.

JACOB
And Benjamin? Give Benjamin some more.

BENJAMIN signals that he doesn't want any more.

JUDAH
He says no thanks.

JACOB
Eat. You've got a long journey ahead of you. –Come here, Benjamin. Come here.

BENJAMIN goes to JACOB, who holds him tight.

Now don't you make trouble for your brothers, you hear? You listen to everything they tell you. And stay close to them. Never lose sight of them, you understand? –Is he nodding?

JUDAH
He's nodding. We'll take good care of him.

JACOB
You'd better. Only why did you have to tell him there was another?

A knock at the door. BENJAMIN runs to look out the window, then looks back, nods.

JUDAH
He's here.

BENJAMIN lets PISCHUK in.

PISCHUK
Evening to you all.

JACOB
Pischuk. I haven't seen you in so long. And now I can just barely.

PISCHUK
Master Jacob.

JACOB
You always took good care of us, Pischuk.

JUDAH
What is it, Pischuk?

PISCHUK
Oustrovski wants more money.

JUDAH
Goddammit. He took his thousand.

PISCHUK
He wants 500 more.

REUBEN
Yes. More. It's not meant to be. We'll get a little ways out of town, into the forest, and there will be soldiers waiting for us.

JUDAH
That's enough. Take them to to the wagon, Pischuk. I'll get the money. I'd left some for him, but now we'll need it.

JACOB
What do I need with money? Pischuk will take good care of me. He'll hide me on his farm. Take it, take it. Now come, one last time, and then no more.

PISCHUK
There will be another.

JUDAH goes. The others embrace JACOB.

REUBEN
Father, your blessing.

JACOB
Go, go.

They go. JUDAH returns.

Give me your hand. Swear to me you'll protect Benjamin. Swear.

JUDAH

I'll bring him back. You won't lose another son. You never have.

JUDAH goes. The wagons are heard moving off. PISCHUK returns.

PISCHUK

Are you ready, Master Jacob?

JACOB

Yes, Pischuk. It's yours now. This house, and everything in it. All the things you kept so well, now yours to keep.

PISCHUK leads JACOB away.

II. ix. Blair's office. 1941.

BLAIR and JOSEPH.

BLAIR

I have here a list of 200 refugee families. Waiting in neutral Sweden for the visas and transport that will bring them to Canada, where they will stay for the duration of the war. The visas have not been issued. Nor will they be, as long as this list remains intact. This office never has, and never will, allow any of its allotted spaces to be dominated by one particular race. There is a quota; the quota will be applied: three-quarters of these families must be removed from the list. *(hands the list to JOSEPH)* Simply place your initials next to those who will be coming; draw a line through those who won't. Make the selections. Or I will make them for you.

JOSEPH flips through, crosses off some names, initials others. BLAIR has a duplicate list.

Give me the names.

JOSEPH

Isaacs. Mendelsohn. Novgorodnik. Goldmann. Dubczanski.

BLAIR

Ah, but there's a problem there, Mr. Taylor. That particular family isn't travelling as a complete unit.

JOSEPH

The father is too ill.

BLAIR

I wasn't referring to the father. It seems that there is a brother, who went some years ago to the United States, and is unaccounted for. I'm afraid that unless he comes forward, he puts his entire family at risk. *(pause)* You'd better cross them off the list. But come, Mr. Taylor, you can still bring 50 families here. Why should only those with connections be saved?

JOSEPH, frozen.

We seem to have reached an impasse, Mr. Taylor. The program is cancelled, pending further review. Let me have the list. I'll need it for my file.

II. x. Prime Minister's Office. 1941.

JOSEPH brings papers for KING to sign.

KING

What have we here? Signing my life away again, am I?

JOSEPH

The usual, Prime Minister. Letters to the temperance union, and various other charities. Letters of sympathy and congratulations to members of and donors to the party. The Hansard speeches of the last several days, you're to sign off.

KING

You've been busy.

JOSEPH

I've checked them myself, sir. No need to bother. The war cabinet meets in an hour.

KING

Of course, of course. Ach. These glasses. These aren't my reading glasses. Would you mind? They're in the desk there.

JOSEPH retrieves the other set of glasses. KING glances through the papers with the first set of glasses, which work perfectly fine. JOSEPH brings the second set.

Ah.

KING begins to sign the papers.

How are your relations with Mr. Blair these days?

JOSEPH

Cordial.

KING

Glad to hear it. You've been working very hard on the refugee file. All sorts of meetings. I understand you've even attended a rally or two.

JOSEPH

Prime Minister, you did ask me to serve as your liaison.

KING

I did, absolutely, and despite what people say I still argue it was the right move.

JOSEPH

People, sir?

KING

Oh, don't you mind about that. People will talk. People have always talked.

> *KING stops signing.*

Joseph, when you came to me, you could barely put one foot in front of the other without tripping. You were angry, condescending, sullen. You've turned into a man before my eyes, a rather dashing one at that – and don't think I haven't heard about your dalliances with young Miss Massey. She's a very pretty girl. Glad to see you won't be following in my shoes there, Joseph.

JOSEPH

Sir, you ought to finish signing the papers.

KING

I'll attend to them. Tell me, Joseph, do you like the influence you enjoy? –Your silence could be construed as an answer.

JOSEPH

I'm not sure how to answer.

KING

Why, honestly, man.

JOSEPH

I never sought to have influence.

KING

Whether you sought it or not isn't the point, dear boy; what you'll do with it is. *(putting his glasses on)* That's better. I can see perfectly well now.

JOSEPH

Sir, those are the same glasses you put on at first.

KING
Some kind of miracle.

KING looks over a letter; signs.

JOSEPH
But there's no need to bother yourself with the letters.

KING
I still need to see the dotted line.

KING signs another letter. Another.

How is that fellow, the one you brought to Kingsmere?

JOSEPH
Well, sir; he's well.

KING
He's a good worker, from the looks of him. Do you know the other day he offered to sew a button for me?

JOSEPH
Did he?

KING
Yes, yes. A button popped off my cardigan, you know; the fellow – what's his name now?

JOSEPH
Simon.

KING
Yes, yes, Simon; only he told me his last name. Bit of a tongue twister, as I recall. Now as to the button, well, it popped off, you see, and this Simon said to me—I can't affect his accent—"Prime Minister, allow me to sew the button for you." You know, it turns out the fellow is a master tailor. Or is it that his father is a master tailor? Well, let's say he comes from a long line of tailors.

JOSEPH
What else did he say?

KING
Oh that was it. Very pleasant it was. I gave him a dollar. Joseph, is there something on your mind? No? You could have fooled me.

KING looks at the pile of letters, puts his pen down. Pause. KING reads the letter at the top of the pile.

I have before me an Order-in-Council. The order calls on the Immigration Branch to issue visas for 200 refugee families stranded in Sweden. I assume from the fact that my name is

on the bottom of this order, that I issued the declaration. I have
to assume it; I certainly don't recall giving the order.

> *Pause.*

JOSEPH

Prime Minister... Prime Minister five years have passed since you
asked me to take on the role of...

> *KING is wagging his finger.*

KING

Your reasons, Joseph.

JOSEPH

The Department of Immigration promised the Jewish
community a number of visas for...

> *KING is again wagging his finger.*

KING

Your reasons.

JOSEPH

This country has a duty, sir, a duty to...

> *JOSEPH stops himself this time. Retrieves photos from his briefcase.*

This is Judah Dubczanski. Here is Reuben Dubczanski. Levi.
Asher. Daniel. Simon. There are more. Here, and here, and here.
They were on the ship that was not permitted to dock. They
were sent back. I sent them back. You asked me to. They are
my brothers. And I am a Jew. I didn't tell you; how could I? You
didn't want Jews on your land; how could you want one beneath
your roof?

KING

But you are. And you'll stay there.

> *KING signs.*

Your family – bring them.

JOSEPH

Thank you, Prime Minister.

II. xi. Kingsmere. The path by the forest.

> *A dining table has been laid out. The brothers enter.*

JUDAH

What's this?

REUBEN
You think it's for us?

SIMON
(appearing) It's for us.

REUBEN
Simon...

> *They embrace.*

Simon, we have seen such things.

SIMON
Are you well? Did Father really not come?

JUDAH
He stayed.

SIMON
And our wives? The children?

REUBEN
We don't know. They separated us, after we got off the ship. They put us on a train, the men in one car, women and children in another. There were soldiers everywhere.

> *BENJAMIN picks up some food.*

JUDAH
Put that down!

SIMON
No, it's alright. Taylor did this. The one who arrested me. He knew it was Rosh Hashanah. He arranged everything.

JUDAH
Were you here the whole time?

SIMON
I was kept in prison three days, then brought here.

JUDAH
What is this place?

SIMON
The Prime Minister lives here. Taylor works for him, follows him everywhere. He made me work here; he'd come around, asking questions. Always the same questions, about the old man, the village, our families, were they well.

JUDAH
Trying to trick you, to trip you up, see if you'd give different answers.

SIMON
No. One time, he spoke in Polish, then never again.

REUBEN
That soldier. He's aiming a rifle right at me.

JUDAH
Stop it.

> *JOSEPH answers. BENJAMIN has disappeared into the forest.*

JOSEPH
Welcome, gentlemen.

JUDAH
Where you take our wives, our children?

JOSEPH
They're safe. You must trust me. Will you trust me?

REUBEN
[What's he saying?]

> *SIMON serves as REUBEN's translator. REUBEN offers the gift.*

JUDAH
Our father sends you this gift. Because he could not come himself. Will you accept it?

JOSEPH
This is from your father?

> *JOSEPH opens the gift. A coat.*

JUDAH
Yes. He is a tailor. We described you to him. Is to be worn as robe. Robe? Material is made of– *(beat)* [You speak Polish? It's made of remainders. He apologises for the material, but this is all he had. He sold his shop, so that we could repay you the money you gave us. The coat is to thank you for your kindness.]

> *JOSEPH has been looking at the coat, walking away from the brothers.*

JOSEPH
I don't understand. You'll have to speak–

> *BENJAMIN appears. BENJAMIN and JOSEPH stand face to face. JOSEPH steps back.*

JUDAH
This is our brother, the one you asked us to bring.

JOSEPH
Benjamin?

JUDAH
Yes.

Silence. Then–

JOSEPH
Please, sit, sit. Oldest to youngest, there are twelve seats. Please.

As they take their seats:

Would one of you like to.... Forgive me... not quite myself tonight... I only wanted to... *(pause)* You've had a long journey... I understand it's your New Year. Simon explained it to me. He said it's a time of renewal, of–.

REUBEN
[What's he saying?]

JUDAH
Will you speak Polish? For my brothers?

JOSEPH
(JOSEPH considers, but continues in English. SIMON translates for REUBEN.) For the coming year. So you have before you apples, to be dipped in honey, to signify hope, hope that the coming year will be both good and sweet. Good and sweet, it is said, because everything that happens is for the good; but not all is sweet.

REUBEN stands.

REUBEN
[I – I want to say something. I want to say, I never meant the boy harm.]

JUDAH
[Sit down.]

REUBEN
[He was a good boy. That's all I wanted to say.]

REUBEN sits. Pause.

JOSEPH
Would one of you say the blessing? The blessing over the wine? There is a blessing, isn't there? I would appreciate–

SIMON
What do you want from us?

JOSEPH
What do I want? ...I want you to say the blessing. That's all. Say the blessing and you can be on your way.

JOSEPH picks up the silver cup. Goes to BENJAMIN.

JUDAH
[He can't speak.]

JOSEPH
No?

JUDAH
I tell you, he's mute.

JOSEPH
Then he should have the cup. So that all the lips that have touched it will speak for him. Only if I put this cup away, it means we won't drink. We won't have the blessing. The book will close, our sins won't be forgiven. Gentlemen, I ask you again and for the last time–

JUDAH
Just let us go. We just want to go. You sent us back to get our brother, he's here. Now to hell with your blessing, let us go.

JOSEPH
Which is his suitcase? His suitcase?

JUDAH points to it.

No. I'll do it. Jews don't work this day. I know all about Jews.

JOSEPH opens the suitcase; slips pamphlets into it.

Oh. Gentlemen. Gentlemen, how you wrong me. I trusted you. I gave you a chance. And you'd make a fool out of me?

"Finds" pamphlets.

What are these? Pamphlets. Writings. Communist writings.

JUDAH
No. It's a mistake.

JOSEPH
Sit down. I'll call the guards. Do you see them? They're all around. In the forest too. Sit down, sit down!

JUDAH
[Benjamin, did you bring these? Did you?]

JOSEPH
Open your suitcases.

JUDAH
No, this is, no, no, listen!

JOSEPH
> You thought because you were coming in under my protection
> that you could bring these lies with you? I gave you a chance,
> and you threw it away. You're not to be trusted. Now open those
> suitcases, open them!

JUDAH
> Mister–

JOSEPH
> I was right to send you back, you're beyond contempt.

REUBEN
> [We're going to die, we're going to die.]

JUDAH
> Mister–

SIMON
> Stop this. You know it's not true.

JOSEPH
> You're exactly what I said–

JUDAH
> No. It's a lie.

JOSEPH
> *(holding up the pamphlets)* Look me in the eye and tell me you
> don't believe what's in here.

JUDAH
> I–

JOSEPH
> That you've never believed it.
>
> > *Pause.*
>
> Guards.

SIMON
> No, wait!

REUBEN
> [God have mercy, God have mercy.]

JUDAH
> Sir–

JOSEPH
> I don't want to hear another word out of you.

REUBEN
> [I never meant him harm, I never meant him harm.]

SIMON

Stop it, stop it!

JUDAH

Listen to me. Yes, we believed – once – but – let me explain, let me explain.

JOSEPH signals for the guards to wait.

Yes, once, we were Communists. But no more. We tried to form a union in our father's shop, but were found out, so had to stop. When war broke out, and the Soviets invaded, they took over our town, and then, yes, we were able to form union. For two years, we could walk the streets of our shtetl, proud to call ourselves Communists. For the first time in our lives, we saw the possibility of creating a new world, a true brotherhood, where all are equal. Then the Germans came, the Russians fled, and we escaped. So we're not Communists any more; we're not Poles any more. We're only Jews, and we have no home. And these pamphlets, I tell you, I don't know how they got into the boy's suitcase, I don't know, I don't know.

JOSEPH

Go on, then. Take your things, take everything, take it, take it!

The brothers begin to pack up. JOSEPH keeps BENJAMIN.

Only this one stays.

JUDAH

No!

JOSEPH

The rest of you go.

JUDAH

No! No! Listen, the boy's a fool. He didn't understand what he was doing. Sir, please. Listen to me. Our father... I promised him... swore to him, that I wouldn't let anything happen to this boy. Please, he has no one to speak for him; let me speak for him; let me speak for him; I'm begging you, let the boy go.

JUDAH gets to his knees. The others follow.

Take me instead. Send me to prison. Only let this one go.

JOSEPH

You would do that?

JUDAH

For my brother, I would do anything.

JOSEPH

And for me? What would you do for me? Am I not your brother?

> *JOSEPH puts on the coat. BENJAMIN is crying.*

[Do I not speak as you speak? I am your brother. I am Joseph. *(to BENJAMIN)* They sent me away. I couldn't understand. Now I do. *(to all)* You sent me away, so that I could save you. Am I not your brother?]

> *JOSEPH holds up the ripped sleeve and piece of lining from the original coat. JUDAH recognises them. He touches JOSEPH's face. They embrace. JOSEPH finds the silver cup. Pours wine into it.*

[I'll tell you everything. Everything… we'll stay up this long night, I'll tell you all. In the morning, I'll take you to your new homes. Not now. Not now. Now we'll drink. We'll drink to those not here. Reuben, our eldest, will you say the blessing?]

> *REUBEN says kiddush. The prayer overlaps with the psalm at the top of the next scene.*

II. xii. The Dubczanski house. 1946.

> *JACOB on his deathbed. PISCHUK reading to him. JOSEPH enters during reading. He carries the coat of remnants.*

PISCHUK

"How long wilt thou forget me, O Lord? For ever? How long wilt thou hide thy face from me? How long shall I take counsel in my soul, having sorrow in my heart daily? How long shall mine enemy be exalted over me? Consider and hear me, O Lord my God: lighten mine eyes, lest I sleep the sleep of death–.

JACOB

Why do you stop, Pischuk?

PISCHUK

A visitor. Come, sir, will you sit?

JACOB

Who is it?

PISCHUK

A man from the Canadian government. He has news of your sons.

> *JACOB waves JOSEPH over.*

JACOB
You know my sons?

JOSEPH
Yes.

JACOB
They left me, you know. Twelve sons I had. Gone. Gone, all gone. And no one to say kaddish for me, just this old Pole. *(waves JOSEPH closer)* His breath stinks.

JOSEPH
Old man, I can take you to your sons.

JACOB
Ah, it's you, then? The angel. Is this to be my reckoning? Come, I'll tell you all I've done. I had a family. Two women I loved. I dreamed one night of multitudes. And multitudes is what I had. Reuben, my eldest, a thinker, and clever, but weak in spirit; nothing is what he came from; nothing is what he'll come to. Simon and Levi, fighters both, men of cruelty; they will seek vengeance for what was done to us, but not against the slaughterers – no, another people will pay the price; Judah will lead them; he is a lion, who sinks his teeth into the neck of his enemies; Benjamin is merciful, and loving; that is why God took from him his speech. The others will follow, after their own kind, in their own way, all, all, but one, who was never meant to follow.

JOSEPH
You mean Joseph?

JACOB
The same. He was taken from me.

JOSEPH
He lives.

JACOB
Liar.

JOSEPH
I can take you to him.

JACOB
No. Is it true?

JOSEPH
His brothers sent him away. They were jealous, so plotted against him. And in so doing, saved themselves.

JACOB

Ah, then Joseph is doomed.

JOSEPH

Doomed?

JACOB

He was all kindness. But to be betrayed by your own brothers will make him bitter til the end of his days.

JOSEPH

He forgave them.

JACOB

Did he know his father lived?

JOSEPH

He did.

JACOB

Then his forgiveness was not genuine. Til the end of his days, Joseph will remember the betrayal. He'll never forgive; he can't; no son of mine could.

JOSEPH

Why do you curse them, your children?

JACOB

I bless them. Give me your hand. Your skin is warm; and mine, so cold. Do you see the well? Do you see that woman there? I'll make her my wife. I fell asleep, with a rock for my pillow. I dreamed of multitudes. And on waking, I knew that my dream was good. Now I sleep again, knowing it was false.

He dies. Pause.

JOSEPH

Not yet, not yet. Take back your curse. One more breath, old man, fill your lungs one last time and remove this curse. Don't tell your Joseph he'll be bitter. I won't be like you. I won't go down to my grave in sorrow and hatred. Speak, old man, speak, speak, speak! ...Your beloved is here, your angel, don't curse me, don't curse me...

Pause.

Pischuk, bring my brothers in. Let them know, Pischuk, he is dead. We'll carry him to the Jewish graveyard.

PISCHUK

It was desecrated during the war; the stones toppled over and broken.

JOSEPH

Then we'll start a new one. Go on, Pischuk; only let me sit here a moment more, watch over him. Give me the burial cloth.

PISCHUK hands JOSEPH the remnants; goes. JOSEPH kisses his father on the forehead. He covers him with the remnants. His brothers enter, surround the body.

He is gone, my brothers, and we are here to comfort his spirit as it ascends. Only I beg you, spirit, fly across the ocean. A child is waiting to be born; descend, spirit, become that child. I will teach that child to speak; I will raise that child with love; we will walk down streets in freedom, seeking not revenge but acts of loving kindness, mending the world, as we ourselves have mended. And do not fear, my brothers; my forgiveness is real, as real as these hands I place in yours. And now come, my brothers, and you, righteous man, take up his body. We will carry him to the burying ground, cleanse him, dress him in sack cloth, return him to the earth, and never forget, but say kaddish until the end of our days.

They lift the body.

THE BROTHERS

(carrying off the body) Yeetgadal v'yeetkadash sh'mey rabbah. B'almah dee v'rah kheer'usey v'yamleekh malkhusei...

The end.

SHINY COAT
PERHAPS BLACK
BENGALINE —
OR A WOOL SATEEN?.
OR A SATIN ?-

JOSEPH'S COAT
FROM JACOB
WITH EXTRAORDINARY
LINING OF REMNANTS

"REMNANTS"-
LININGS — USE LC
OLD TIES PERHAPS
THE BLACK THING?

REMNANTS
TARRAGON 2003.

Original costume sketch for Joseph
by Charlotte Dean.

Notes on Remnants (A Fable)

It wasn't always a fable. Or maybe it was, and I didn't realise it until it was all over – which is why I'm adding the words in parenthesis now.

I.i. *Remnants* went through a series of false starts, and might never have been written at all were it not for a threatened lawsuit. These missteps included my adaptation of the book *None Is Too Many*, a factual account of how Canada closed its doors to Jewish immigration between the years 1933-1948. I wrote it as a docudrama for the Winnipeg Jewish Theatre and Manitoba Theatre Centre, which produced it to no great acclaim in 1997. Figuring I'd squandered an opportunity, I took my adaptation to the Canadian Stage Company, where I tried unsuccessfully to fashion it into a play. My third run at the material came when, on the verge of abandoning the revised version, I realised that the historical record needed to serve the drama, not the other way around. Several years earlier I'd participated in a composer-librettist workshop in Toronto, during which I'd written lyrics for a short scene (with the wonderful and late lamented Milton Barnes) based on the biblical story of Joseph and his brothers. The characters were Joseph, now a dream therapist in contemporary Toronto, and Judah, a man suffering from a recurring nightmare in which seven emaciated men dine at a table laden with food, but gain no weight. Joseph realises that the man is his brother, from whom Joseph had become separated as a child in Poland, and who, until that moment, Joseph believed had perished in the Second World War. I'd thought to expand the idea one day. I now had my chance.

Canadian Stage was on board for one more workshop, during which the story and characters began to take shape. Parallels between the Bible story and the historical record quickly emerged. The biblical Joseph and his family of shepherds became a family of tailors, a likely occupation for the Jews of Eastern European shtetls. The Pharaoh who sought clues to the meaning of his strange dreams easily became

Prime Minister William Lyon Mackenzie King, who liked to hold seances at his country estate, and believed that his dreams were messages sent by his loved ones from the great beyond. Nor was it a stretch to find an equivalent to the famine, what with drought, famine and hordes of insects having destroyed Canada's wheat crops during the Great Depression. The first draft of what I was calling *Remnants* fell into place relatively quickly; what I didn't expect was that the production would, too.

Here's the thumbnail: I'd been writing a play about Marshall McLuhan for Richard Rose, then artistic director of Necessary Angel Theatre Company. That play was coming along nicely, to the point where Richard was set to direct its premiere at the Tarragon Theatre in September 2003. But then the McLuhan family read a draft of the play and hated it. ("It's libelous, slanderous, misrepresentative, filled with nasty language and open to lawsuits," one member of the family told me.) A decision (of which I was a part) was made to shelve the McLuhan play and replace it with something else – of mine. I suggested a tenth anniversary production of *Three in the Back, Two in the Head*, the first play of mine to be done at the Tarragon and, like the McLuhan play, a work that had been commissioned and developed by Richard through Necessary Angel. But he had another idea. "What about *Remnants?*" he asked me. I wasn't sure. Neither was he, not completely. He'd liked the first draft, even though it was half-formed and some scenes were written out in the manner of a film treatment:

SWEAT SHOP.
Joseph, on the floor of the shop. It's loud and hot. Joseph works hard; with his training, he figures out a way for the shop to be more productive. He comes to the attention of the owner, Hal Pottinger.

AN OFFICE.
Pottinger, owner of the sweat shop, offers Joseph a foreman's job. Tells Joseph to be on the lookout for Communists -- trying to set up a union, they've infiltrated the shop. "These people don't appreciate what we do for them." Joseph promises to keep a watch out.

Mrs Pottinger comes in, takes instant liking to Joseph.

Now he wanted to read it again.

When I'd handed Richard that first draft a year or so earlier, he'd quickly peeked at the first page, laughed and said "Good first line." I think it contains the only curse word in the entire play – what lobby signs refer to as "Language." I aimed to make the dialogue sound different than the everyday, steer it away from what's normally (and rather unhelpfully) called naturalism, to make it seem as though we were listening to a translation of sorts, that we were in a different world.

> JUDAH. Burn that ticket and burn that goddamn letter. Nobody's going anywhere. The old man'd cut off his left arm before he let a single one of his sons go. Screwed our mother to death to fill his shop with cheap labour. And there sits the seed of his union with the little whore who took her place.

Richard called the morning after we buried the McLuhan play to say that he now wanted to do *Remnants*, and in the same slot. Rehearsals were to begin August 18. It was now May.

Canadian Stage graciously—or perhaps gratefully—relinquished its rights. I then spent the rest of May and all of June not writing the second draft. By July, when we had to start our already belated casting, I still hadn't made much progress. Richard, by contrast, was well on his way to conceptualising the production, which he explained to me in an email:

> I'm visually playing around with the idea of seeing and not seeing. Actors walk into blackness and then into light while the scene goes on. Sort of trying to follow a notion of Joseph's sight or seeing as distinct from the blindness of the other characters. Graeme [Thomson, set & lighting designer] was talking about the illumination behind heads in ancient paintings – moments of visions as bright, illuminated moments and it incorporates elements of black magic; e.g., suits floating in the air and in Joseph's mind, interrupted by Judah's "Look, it's the little shit." Judah, when he goes to assault Joseph, steps into the dark and only when Judah turns to him before "Hello, Judah" do the lights come up on him. I am also thinking very pictorially, with scenes very much like still images or tableau to tableau within scenes. Still all images or stuff comes through suitcases.

The amazing thing is that it all worked, and beautifully. The suitcases doubled not only as practical props, but as whatever else we needed them to be. The various bags, trunks and boxes were arranged and dismantled and rearranged a dozen or more times to become, as needed, seats on a train, sewing machines, a park bench, a stone wall, a pathway, a dinner table, church pews, and all manner of desks, podiums and chairs. This rather ingenious system gave the piece a thrilling theatricality, in which the world seemed to be falling apart and rebuilding itself constantly. It was a solution born of a dilemma (too little time, an ever-changing script) but it also proved that sometimes the best solutions really do rise out of adversity.

As enamoured as I was, and remain, of the production, the moment I liked least was the opening. On Graeme Thomson's simple black box set lay Joseph, eyes closed, caught in a spotlight. The stage directions call for him to be "lost in thought," which is to say, awake, trying to understand his troubling dream of the previous night. Along come two of his rough-and-tumble brothers to interrupt his thoughts and force him to reveal the content and meaning of his dream, thus beginning the chain of events that will end in another land thirteen years later. And because this is a fable, there's little time, and sometimes no time at all, for the characters to stop and analyse their "situation," to ponder and pontificate. We are telling a story, and leaving it to the observers to find their own meanings, to be their own dream analysts. The production was designed, literally, to look and feel like a dream, from the lighting to the sound to the fine mesh scrim that separated the audience from the actors, making them seem present but distant, as people often appear in dreams.

Richard wanted to depict Joseph's dream, even as he was having it (hence the discovery of Joseph, asleep). To that end, thirteen suits of various shapes and sizes were rigged up, some of them suspended in midair, several of them rising from the large trunk that sat centrestage. Then, Joseph awakens and—poof—the suits vanish. Sounds fine in theory, but in practice, the effect never worked to anyone's satisfaction, including Richard and Graeme's, who spent a lot of time trying to find just the right combination of lighting effect and timing that would turn the whole thing into a sort of *coup de théâtre*. Then came an image that would be repeated throughout the production: a lineup, this one of men leaving the post office. It didn't read that way to me, and the subsequent slow-paced reading of the letter only compounded what had become, to me, a long, drawn-out opening sequence – not quite the brisk, lapel-grabbing opening that I thought I'd written. But a director has his own sense of a play's rhythms and balances, and no one, not even the guy who wrote it, can shake his faith in it.

I.ii. A scene that kept on changing. It was originally set in the woods just outside of town, with Joseph showing Benjamin how to create a Golem (a man-made creature, a protector, composed of sand and brought to life with magic spells) but that was when Joseph was secretly studying the mystic traditions of kabbalah, and was to be guided on his journey by spirits. The rather obvious intent of the scene was to show how much Benjamin depended upon Joseph, and their deep love for one another. But that's the problem with writing a scene where you're trying to depict an intent – you get the intent, and very little else.

I tried for some time to work metaphysics into the play, to suggest that the world was alive with something beyond the corporeal, that it

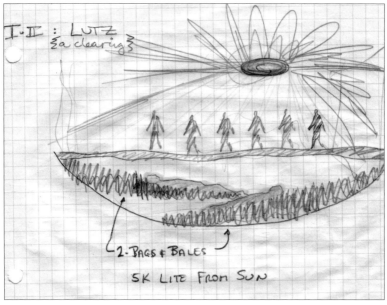

Original lighting design sketch for I.ii Luzniki
by Graeme Thomson.

was infused with the spirits of the dead, who could speak to Joseph in various human, animal and even seemingly inanimate guises. Alon Nashman, who is something of a fount of information on matters Hebraic, gave me a Talmudic version of the Joseph story, from Louis Ginsberg's "Legends of the Jews." Here, the mystical elements of the story are brought out as in no other version I've read. There are talking birds and babies who suddenly speak as adults – it's magical realism before the term was invented, and all of it in keeping with a story that, after all, centres on a boy who correctly interprets dreams. After reading Ginsberg's take, I revisited my own stalled attempts to weave the spiritual into the everyday, but with the exception of the dream sequences it all seemed shoehorned in. So there would be no Golem-making, no kabbalah, and definitely no talking birds.

It was Richard who suggested moving the scene from the woods to the synagogue, where it began to find its place in the story. It allowed us to see the entire family (or as many of the family members as there were actors to play them, the other brothers being implicit). Even after changing the setting, the scene kept going through revisions through the preview period. Only by the fourth preview (of six), with the addition of Joseph's speech about becoming "a great scholar," was the text finalised. A small change, but it hinted at Joseph's combination of naivete and self-importance, two of the qualities that so enraged his brothers. It would have been easy to make Joseph a brat, and therefore an understandable target of his brother's wrath. The challenge throughout the first act was to create a drama out of a seemingly—seemingly—passive character who, through no fault of his own, finds himself an outcast who must struggle to not only survive but to understand why he was cast out. Joseph bubbles away beneath the surface, a difficult character to grasp (and to play) in the absence of interior monologues. We have to rely, for the most part, on what is said to him and about him to get a sense of who he is.

I.iii. The first scene I wrote for what would become *Remnants*. Very little changed. Jacob's second wife was part of the scene, but I finally accepted the fact that women had very little to do with this story. It wasn't for lack of trying, and it wasn't until I had to deliver the production draft—when tough decisions have to be made—that I decided to make it an all-male revue. In the original tale, there are two female characters: Tamar, daughter-in-law of Judah; and Potiphar's wife, whose attempt to seduce Joseph results in his being thrown into prison, a necessary step on his fall and consequent rise to power. But the Tamar subplot never made it into the play, and Potiphar's wife presented her own dramaturgical problems, which are addressed below.

I.iv. Richard wanted the violence to be as visceral as possible, so that Joseph (and the audience) would remember the pain he suffered at the hands of his brothers. Charlotte Dean, the costume designer, was asked to come up with a protective undercoat that would absorb the blows Joseph was to receive at the hands of Simon, who was to use a riding crop to repeatedly whip Joseph into confessing that he'd spied for Jacob. Charlotte describes the vest:

> It was built out of two different weights of leather, with blue, high density foam sandwiched between them. The leather had been spec'd by the fight guy. To fasten it securely, it had wide (like two-inch) velcro enclosures, which closed it like a wraparound vest. Because of the movement, we then had to mount it onto bike shorts, in order for it not to ride up, which would have exposed the kidneys to harm. Bit of a challenge for getting into. And Dmitry [Chepovetsky]'s costumes had to be adjusted up a size for allowance. There was always a certain amount of hunching when he bent his head down, which made it all a bit growly. It probably weighed about five pounds.

Since Joseph is in every scene, there was no opportunity for Dmitry to get rid of his body armour. He soldiered on, all through rehearsals. By the time previews came around, the normally cool Tarragon Mainspace felt like a sauna with the addition of up to 200 bodies, and Dmitry's suffering was very real indeed. Richard reblocked the scene, so that Joseph's Amazing Leather-covered Undercoat could be dispensed with altogether. Now, instead of Simon landing blow after blow on Joseph's back, he used the riding crop to strangle Joseph. It was vicious, memorable, a vast improvement over the original blocking. And there was one other gain: Dmitry said he felt much freer without the vest, and his performance proved it. He seemed more in command of his role and, no longer encumbered, he became the driving force of the play.

I.vi. Actors and directors are notorious for ignoring stage directions. (See my notes to I.i. for evidence.) Perhaps that's why I tend to write so few of them. Here, though, Richard did try to honour my original call to have Joseph leap out of the cart, sprain his ankle and then be lugged back by Pischuk. In the end, it all looked so phony, so stagey, so completely at odds with everything around it, that I only had to see it once to agree that it had to go.

I.vii. A scene that took forever to get right on the page. It should have all been so simple: Joseph arrives in a new country (not even the one he thought he was going to) without proper documentation, and has to explain his way in. I tried having him play mute (a trick he would have learned by observing Benjamin), but that fell flat. I tried having him get caught with Communist Party literature, but that seemed both unlikely and forced.

One day I came into rehearsal, having sent in the latest version of the scene the day before. The boys had been working on it all morning. "Okay," announced Richard, "let's show Jason what we've got." What followed was a skillfully executed, tightly choreographed bit of business in which Joseph was accused of being a spy, hauled off to an interrogation room, and berated to the point of tears over his affiliations and intentions. I could see that the actors were quite pleased with the results, though I think they were also anxious to move on. To me, though, it felt less like an improvement than an improv. I decided to take one more run at it, returning to a character I'd grown very fond of, and dependent on – Max Becker. Max emerged in an early workshop and refused to go away. Here's one of my first sketches of him:

Halifax. Outside the Immigration Centre.

BECKER. Somebody meeting you?

JOSEPH. I don't know. I don't think so.

BECKER. You don't know? Just starting out, are you? Come over to make your fortune?

JOSEPH. Not really.

BECKER. Well, I did. Name's Englebrot, Max Englebrot. Actually, it's "Becker" now. Max Becker. See, the immigration guy, he looks at my name, he says, "Englebrot? What's that?" Like he did with you, see. Anyways, we go through this whole thing, and he finally asks me, he says, like he did with you, he goes, "What did your father do?" And I go, "He's a baker," right? Only it comes out "Becker," on account of my accent, see? So he goes, "Becker, Max Becker." How do you like that, huh? Aw, not that I mind, Joe – mind if I call you Joe? I don't mind, Joe, cause, I mean, here I am, I'm making a fresh start, so what the hell, eh, might as well have a fresh name. "Becker," ha! That's a laugh. Wait'll I tell the folks back home. Say, you got any cigarettes there, Joey?

JOSEPH. I don't smoke.

BECKER. Well that's a shame-and-a-half. How about money, you bring any money?

JOSEPH. Yes.

He digs out some notes.

BECKER. Zlotys! Ha ha ha! Joey, you kill me, you do. Brings over Zlotys! Yeah – ha ha! A lot of zlotys. Listen, fella, I don't know too much about this Canada place, but I don't think zlotys is exactly the national currency, know what I mean?

In one draft he'd had a very significant role, showing Joseph around the streets of Toronto, taking him, at one point, to a diner that was off-limits to Jews. But it had rather little to do with Joseph's story, and too much to do with the history of anti-Semitism in Canada. Given the play's antecedents, it was a history I didn't want the story to get bogged down in. Max then turned into a different sort of guide, a supernatural one, who would accompany Joseph on his journey through the new world. It took several runs at that before I settled on Max being a representative figure of the time: a European Communist, a Jew who has come to the new world to help spread the doctrine. Taking my cue from Genesis, I thought to make Max a slave trader, who brings Joseph to Egypt (or, in this case, Toronto) and puts him to work in the house of Potiphar (the factory of Pottinger). But I could find nothing in the historical record to suggest that there were slave traders. It would be true to say that the needle trade made slaves of its employees, which is more to the point, but to suggest that representatives of the garment industry grabbed immigrants as they stepped off the boat would not only be inaccurate but—the worse sin—melodramatic. So Max became a union organiser, and this too served the play better, since it resonated with Joseph's earlier experiences in Paddan, where his own brothers had tried to form a union. Nice idea, but it all seemed too schematic when it came to be written. The union story is there, but subordinated to the larger story of Joseph and his brothers.

I.viii. One of the difficulties in telling a story so laden with dreams is that listening to them can be about as thrilling as watching paint crack. So I tried to present each dream in a different form than the last. This scene, which has no parallel in the Bible story, was my way of getting inside Joseph's head, showing us that his past is weighing heavily on his mind. I'd thought to apply the technique more thoroughly through the play, but soon discovered that overuse was overkill. (A number of dream sequences ended up being cut in rehearsal or during preview week.) The scene succeeded in keeping the audience off-balance, not knowing it was a dream until very near the end; but you can only do that once for it to be effective. King's dream (at the end of this act) is somewhat similar in approach, but has a different way in, a different tone and feeling.

I.ix. The first production draft, which I felt at the time of writing nailed this part of the story, featured a very long version of this scene, in which Max went on at length about the union struggle and the importance of Joseph's participation. Max continued to evolve, and was such an invigorating presence—played with great humour and mystery by Alon—that he took over every scene he was in, upstaging Joseph, taking the story down a different path. With more time, I might have gone down that path. Not this time. Max's role shrank very quickly and dramatically after the first table-read. Long speeches were cut; in the end, Max's role as an agitator was limited to a couple of lines, and even then they had to compete with the cranked-up sound of a hundred sewing machines.

The scene is set in the cutting room of Pottinger & Sons, and the cutting room floor is precisely where so many ideas ended up. Here, for example, is one attempt to present the political and social realities facing Joseph (Max is called David, for a reason which escapes me):

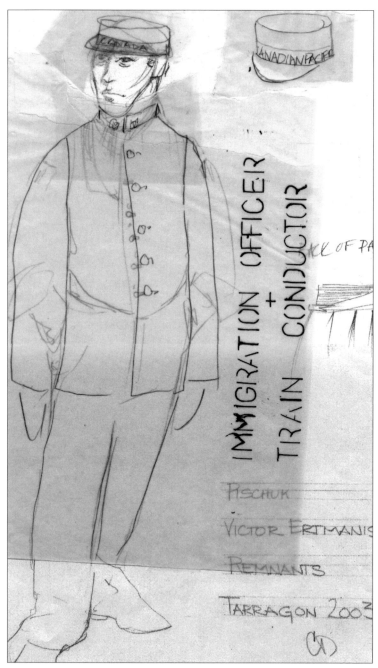

Original costume sketch for Immigration Officer and Train Conductor
by Charlotte Dean.

JOSEPH. My father was told he'd be a great man. In the end he was a tailor trying to make ends meet for a large family. In our own community he was respected, but in the larger world he was a speck of dust in the eye of the goy. Me, I was promised greatness, too. In my dreams my brothers were going to bow down to me.

DAVID. Instead they sold you down the river. Or should I say across the ocean. Listen – you think you're the only one ever dreamed like that? I mean take a look around, Joe. I guarantee you everybody else in this room once dreamt great things for themselves. Only it didn't work out that way – why? Because they never had the opportunity is why.

JOSEPH. There are rules against talking during shift.

DAVID. Of course there are, and you know why? Cause Pottinger knows that talk is dangerous. Talk is how ideas spread, and right now we've got an idea so hot it's gonna burn down everything in its path.

JOSEPH. You're only interested in destroying things.

DAVID. Only to build new things – new, and better. Why won't you come to a meeting?

JOSEPH. I know what's going to be said. I'm not interested.

DAVID. How could you not be interested? How could you not want to make things better? I mean are things so good around here you don't think they could stand a little improving?

JOSEPH. It isn't my fight.

DAVID. I suppose you think god's gonna make everything better, huh? Yeah, the same god that sent you your dreams of power. You think that's how it is, boyo? You think things work out cause they've been meant to work out? Or do you think maybe human beings have something to do with it? You think maybe there's such a thing as "will" and "courage"?

Bell rings for end of shift. Enter Pottinger, with several ladies.

POTTINGER. Now here is the area of the shop where the clothes are packaged for distribution. And here are two of my finest workers. Ladies, Joseph is, in some ways, a typical employee here at Pottinger & Sons. A recent immigrant, or should I say, fairly recent immigrant. Joseph, how long have you been in this country?

JOSEPH. Four years, Mr. Pottinger.

POTTINGER. Four years, ladies. And in that time, this dedicated young man—a hard worker and, ladies I'm sure you'll agree, a strapping young lad—has risen through the ranks. And why is that? Because he has a purpose in life, which is to do good work, honest work, to live his life as one of god's humble, devoted servants. Now

I know, ladies, that there's been a lot of trouble in some of the other factories with the Reds trying to take advantage of the recent economic downturn to stir up trouble—Eaton's for example has had a bit of a rough go—but here at Pottinger's, my employees know that their needs come first. Our motto is "a happy worker is a productive worker." Isn't that right, Joseph?

JOSEPH. Is right, Mr. Pottinger.

POTTINGER. You mean to say, "That is right." You see, ladies, Joseph is still grappling with the finer points of the language. That's one of the reasons I invited you here.

FIRST WOMAN. Mr. Pottinger, the work here is simply outstanding. Look, girls, double stitching.

POTTINGER. That's right, ladies. Here at Pottinger and Sons, we don't believe in skimping on material. Our clothes are not only fashionable, but made to last.

SECOND WOMAN. Mr. Pottinger, hasn't the union gained a bit of a foothold at Tip Top Tailors?

POTTINGER. Of course, but as I'm sure you know, Tip Top is Jew-owned. We all know that Jews are Communistic by nature. That's another thing about Joseph – another thing that sets him apart. He's a Jew, but he's never once shown any Communistic tendencies. I can tell you, it's earned him the spite of his fellow workers. Well there's a price to be paid for courage. – Oh, Joseph, be sure to stop by my office later, there's a good lad. – Now, ladies, if you'll come this way, I'll show you the sorting floor...

Pottinger and the Ladies head off. One remains.

CHRISTIAN LADY. Young man, I wonder if you'd be good enough to take my card. My name is Julia Kaye. I'm with the Christian Welcome Mission. It's such a shame a young man such as yourself will find his opportunities limited as a result of his, well, persuasion.

JOSEPH. Please?

CHRISTIAN LADY. Our group meets every Wednesday night at St. Luke's on Adelaide Street. We welcome new members. We welcome those who want to atone. We can help you find your way, young man. Well, I should join the other ladies. I'd say "God be with you," but I just know he already is.

She goes.

DAVID. She's right, you know. There's no future here for the Jew. If that's the way you see yourself. You have to cast off those old clothes, Joseph, get rid of all the superstitions. Come and join the Brotherhood.

In the first draft, I had Joseph working as a butler in the home of Mr. & Mrs. Pottinger, owners of a clothing factory. One night, bolstered by drink and Joseph's beauty, Mrs. Pottinger attempts to seduce him. I ended up cutting the scene (and the character), after failing to convince Richard to have Mrs. Pottinger played by a man. (Both Alon and Victor Ertmanis—who played King—read the role when we were auditioning potential Josephs. They were pretty good, too, and after all this was storytelling theatre, so why not have one of our guys step into a dress and wear a wig for one scene?) In the end, the arguments against Mrs. Pottinger went beyond stunt casting. The fact is that I couldn't find a satisfactory way to end the scene, which is often a telltale sign that a scene doesn't fit. Having Mr. Pottinger seduce Joseph made much more sense: it advanced the story, brought into play the idea of loyalty and sacrifice, and made the scene darker, which is never a bad thing. A dramaturgical trifecta. But I still regret having to cut it.

MRS. POTTINGER. Joseph? Is that you?

JOSEPH. Yes.

MRS. POTTINGER. Would you come in here a moment? — There you are. How was your walk?

JOSEPH. Good. Was good.

MRS. POTTINGER. It was good.

JOSEPH. Yes. Okay. It was good.

MRS. POTTINGER. Are you alright, Joseph? You seem somewhat discombobulated.

JOSEPH. Please?

MRS. POTTINGER. You seem upset.

JOSEPH. No. I must shluff – mm, sleep, yes?

MRS. POTTINGER. What did you call it? "Shluff," oh, that's darling. What language is that?

JOSEPH. Is – Polish.

MRS. POTTINGER. Of course. Joseph, you really must teach me some more of your language, I think it's just delicious, I really do.

JOSEPH. Okay, missus.

MRS. POTTINGER. Joseph?

JOSEPH. Missus?

MRS. POTTINGER. Be a dear and get me another martini?

JOSEPH. Of course.

MRS. POTTINGER. Oh, and Joseph? Joseph?

JOSEPH. Missus?

MRS. POTTINGER. Pour one for yourself.

JOSEPH. Please?

MRS. POTTINGER. It'll warm you up.

Joseph goes about making Mrs. Pottinger's martini.

MRS. POTTINGER. Yes. Getting cold, isn't it? And it gets so dark so early this time of year. It's dreadful, it really is. *(pause)* Mr. Pottinger called before. He's staying the night in Ottawa. – Joseph? Did you hear me?

JOSEPH. Sorry?

MRS. POTTINGER. Really, Joseph, where's your mind tonight? I said Mr. Pottinger is staying the night in Ottawa. So there won't be any need to turn down his bed. Just mine. How are those martinis coming?

Joseph shakes the container.

MRS. POTTINGER. I just love that sound. – He said—Mr. Pottinger, that is—he said he likely wouldn't be back until quite late tomorrow, Joseph. I told him to stay just as long as he wished. They're all quite concerned about wheat prices. I don't really understand any of that business. Something to do with—what is it now?— Oh, what was that word he used? Oh yes, a "glut." Isn't that a funny word? "Glut." Almost sounds like "glug," doesn't it? – Joseph?

JOSEPH. Yes, missus.

MRS. POTTINGER. Now, Joseph, you're really beginning to upset me. I'm trying to have a conversation with you. Really, you've got to improve your English.

Joseph hands her the martini.

MRS. POTTINGER. Two olives. Just the way I like it. *(drinks)* Wonderful. Mm. Oh, it just goes down, and down, and down. But where is yours?

JOSEPH. Not for me.

MRS. POTTINGER. Oh nonsense.

JOSEPH. Really, no.

MRS. POTTINGER. I insist. Here, take a sip of mine. Go on.

Joseph takes a sip.

MRS. POTTINGER. Do you like it?

JOSEPH. Is okay.

MRS. POTTINGER. "Is okay." Honestly, Joseph. Now an olive. Come on. Sit. Sit. I'm going to feed you one. After all, why should you do all the work? Mm? Do you know, I was reading the most fascinating thing in one of the magazines the other day, something about how in Roman times, there would be a carnival once a year

Original lighting design sketch for I.vii Canadian Immigration
by Graeme Thomson.

where—now what was it?—the masters would be slaves for a day, and the slaves would be masters. I think that's a marvelous idea, Joseph, don't you? *(She rubs her foot along his leg.)* Masters and slaves... slaves and masters... when you get right down to it, Joseph, we're all just people, aren't we? Oh, some of us are rotten to the core, there's no doubt about that, while others are absolute saints. But even the rotters have their good points, and saints can be corrupted. What's your opinion?

Joseph says nothing.

MRS. POTTINGER. I so want to kiss you, Joseph. Don't you want to kiss me?

JOSEPH. Please. I go now.

MRS. POTTINGER. Only if you kiss me. Once. In a friendly way.

Joseph gives her a quick peck.

MRS. POTTINGER. Surely we're better friends than that.

She smothers him in a kiss, pushes his shirt up, kisses his chest.

MRS. POTTINGER. You're so beautiful... I've had my eyes on you from the beginning...

JOSEPH. Please...

MRS. POTTINGER. Shh.... Shh.... You don't need to speak for this part, Joseph. My darling Joseph.

She rips his shirt off.

MRS. POTTINGER. Oops. I think you lost a button.

Kisses his chest.

MRS. POTTINGER. Mm... your skin... so soft...

Sound of a door opening.

MRS. POTTINGER. Oh god.

MR. POTTINGER. *(off)* Doris?

She jumps off the couch, hanging onto Joseph's shirt.

MRS. POTTINGER *(screams)* Ahhhhhhh! Help! Helllllllllp!

I.x. The song at the top of this scene was sung by Nazi sympathisers at the time in the streets of Toronto. I changed a few words.

I.xi-xiii. Alon sang The Carter Family's "No Depression In Heaven," which I found on a collection of American folk songs, during the transition from the park to the train. Graeme built a stunning light cue to suggest the exterior of the train, while shadowy figures sat hunched in the gloom. The lyrics:

> For fear the hearts of men are failing,
> For these are latter days we know.
> The Great Depression now is spreading,
> God's word declared it would be so.
>
> I'm going where there's no depression,
> To the lovely land that's free from care.
> I'll leave this world of toil and trouble,
> My home's in Heaven, I'm going there.

The work camp scenario seemed the perfect match to the prison setting of the Bible story. In one draft, there was more talk of Communist infiltration, but it became clear that less of that was more. The simple equation was this: the more time spent with other characters, the less there would be to spend with Joseph. As rich as the history of the time is, the central figure here has to be Joseph. Everything and everyone else is secondary. I was writing far too much material, scenes expanding beyond their needs, threatening to push Joseph and his struggle right out of the picture. And nothing took up more of my time than the story of Mackenzie King.

I.xiv. King fascinated me, and I made the mistake of trying to work that fascination into the play. I'd read that his diaries, which he maintained from early in his life until just a few days before he died, contained numerous references to his spiritual beliefs, along with details of the seances he routinely held at Kingsmere, his estate. What I didn't know was that dreams were even more important to him than his pathetic attempts to communicate with his beloved dead mother through a psychic. The diaries are available online, an advancement in research that is both a blessing (if you know what you're looking for) and a curse (if you don't know when to stop). The diaries are also searchable, and when I looked up the key word "dream" I got 512 hits. The fact is I didn't need to use King's own dreams, since I knew I was going to use a variation on the Pharaoh's dreams. I read portions of his diaries to get a sense of the man, his voice, his beliefs, his character. My plan was to look at a few of the entries and get back to writing the play. But I got hooked. I couldn't stop reading about the man, his impressions of the times, of the people in his life – from his endless supply of servants, to the rich and famous, to several women who were

Original costume sketch for Joseph's coat
by Charlotte Dean.

the objects of much unrequited love. (He remained a bachelor until the end.) And I haven't even mentioned the dogs, of which there were three, each named for its predecessor, thusly: Pat, Pat II, Pat III.

Richard kept trying to steer me away from making too much of King. But I not only fell in love with the character, I became deeply attached to the actor playing him. Victor Ertmanis is one of the most skillful actors in the country; possessed of a rich bass voice, he commands attention. He's one of those actors who's wonderful to have in the rehearsal room – completely committed to the play, and without a trace of an ego. He also seemed to get King from the first time he spoke the man's words.

For all these reasons, I began writing long, involved scenes for King – an introduction to him, for example, that went on for five minutes (an eternity on stage) but had, it turned out, nothing to do with the play, and everything to do with my sudden infatuation with a character and an actor.

The first time I wrote King into *Remnants*, he was discovered mid-scene, speaking about his dreams and listening to Joseph's interpretation. I remember watching Victor during auditions, reading with potential Josephs, and thinking that it seemed right to meet King in this way. No introduction seemed necessary. Yet I spent weeks expanding the scene, adding in new characters, new beats – all that research! Then, in previews, I began to chop away at it all, until I finally came back full circle to the way I'd first written it. There's a lot to be said about instinct.

II.i. We cut a dream sequence in previews, the same dream Joseph has later, in scene six. Placed at the top of the act, followed by the seance, it made for a slow opening. The scene—in which Joseph imagines his brothers in great danger—also seemed too on-the-nose, easy to interpret, not very dreamlike at all. Once it was gone, the second act tightened up considerably, finally taking shape. I've seen it happen time and again: make the right cut, and everything falls into place. (The opposite is also true – make the wrong cut, and things fall apart very quickly.)

Joseph had originally stood by in silence for much of the scene, but Richard and Dmitry convinced me that Joseph needed to make his presence felt. After all, here he was, three years on, confidante to King, and confident in his position – he didn't have to stand there and be mocked by the servants. Yes, there's strength in silence, but the time had come for Joseph to give as good as he got. (I ended up rewriting his retort to Jack half-a-dozen times.) There was some criticism from members of the Toronto Drama Bench that having the story leap forward by several years during the intermission was an easy route to take, that we should instead have seen the transition from Joseph-the-humble to Joseph-the-power broker. I can't think of anything that would have been easier to show – or duller: scenes of Joseph at university, or having his suits measured, or learning to speak English, or falling in love with a nice Canadian girl. To me, there was power in seeing Joseph transformed – and then plunging him into a crisis. The rest is implied. This is a fable, after all, not a work of stubbornly detailed realism.

II.ii. Frederick Blair is an historical figure, and the lone holdover from my adaptation of *None Is Too Many*. (King also put in an appearance there, but as a caricature. After being told of a sign on a Toronto beach that read, "No dogs or Jews," the dog-loving King paused, then asked, incredulous, "No dogs?") That Blair also has no direct parallel in the

Joseph story forms the third point of the Bermuda Triangle into which his scenes kept threatening to disappear. An early version of this scene had Joseph standing by in silence (again) while Blair explained the refugee situation to King, who was being fitted for a new suit. What a mess it was, and what a bigger mess I made of it, rewriting it almost past the point of comprehension. Write down a few words in pencil, then erase them. Write them again in the same spot; erase them again. Rewrite, erase, rewrite, erase. Pretty soon, you won't be able to make out the new words at all. That, in a sense, is what happened to this scene. Jerry Franken, who played Blair, never quit on it, and in fact kept at Richard and me to knock some dramatic sense into the two Blair scenes. I was a little nervous about throwing substantive changes at Jerry, having never worked with him before. Some actors don't take well to late-breaking revisions; Jerry took them very well. He was a marvel on stage and off: selfless; an inspiration.

II.iii. A scene that needed very few revisions after the first draft. I switched around a few lines, nothing much. Once the boys started to play it, it was clear that they had plenty to work with. (I'd thought perhaps it was underwritten.)

I loved looking at the scene, which was beautifully conceived and executed by the design team – Graeme, Charlotte and Todd Charlton (sound). It achieved everything Richard set out in his July email—"scenes very much like still images"—and everything I'd hoped to do by placing the biblical tale in a contemporary setting. I remember speaking to Graeme on break one afternoon, and telling him how I felt about the look and feel of the scene. He took a drag on his cigarette, exhaled and, allowing himself a slight grin, said, "Yeah, it's my favourite cue."

II.iv. Richard wanted Jason Jazrawy (Simon) to play the scene in fear and apprehension. He did—clutching his bag to his chest—but only up until the moment when Francis offered up a hand in friendship. During the first pass at putting the scene on its feet, Jason went to shake Francis' hand. Richard asked him not to. Simon was cut off from everything he knew: nothing would be familiar or calming to him, not even a proffered hand, which, after all, could be reaching out to take something, like that clutched bag. Jason countered. He said it was clear that the guy wanted to shake his hand. Richard: "You can't understand a word he's saying. How do you know he wants to shake your hand?" Jason wouldn't budge. Richard popped up from his seat, went over to Kyle Horton (Francis), whispered something in his ear, and had the guys do the scene again. This time, when Kyle began to speak, it was in gibberish. Oh, it was the text, line for line, but it was coming out as some strange, made-up language. (Kyle, a brilliantly funny and understated actor, seemed to be channelling the spirit of Sid Caesar.) Jason's fear and apprehension seemed more tangible now. This time, when Kyle reached out his hand, Jason was taken aback. It was clear from his reaction that he had no idea why the hand was being offered. The scene finished. Jason looked over at Richard, and with a sheepish grin on his face, said, "Got it."

II.vii. Max's return. The original setting for Max's confrontation with Joseph was Kingsmere, but as Richard pointed out, it seemed awfully easy for Max to get there undetected. He suggested moving the scene to King's church, which would give us a new, unusual setting, and point rather starkly to Joseph's changed conditions.

We also added, at the last minute, Joseph receiving a note to the effect that war had been declared, which gives the scene—for Joseph, at least—an added urgency.

II.viii. When Alon came in to help with the auditions, he asked if he could sing a song that might be of use to us. It was called "Yam Lid," or "Song of the Sea," and he performed it *a capella*, in Yiddish, for me and Richard in the empty space of the Tarragon's main stage. He seemed to be there and a million miles away at the same time. It's always a treat to watch Alon build a role, almost by stealth, and then, having settled on it, watch him deepen it. "Song of the Sea" was written in Hebrew by the 12th century poet Judah ha-Levi, then translated into Yiddish by the early 20th century writer Chaim Nachman Bialik. The first lines, in English, are "I have forgotten all my loved ones, I have left my own home. I've abandoned myself to the sea: carry me, Sea, to my mother's bosom!" Alon's gorgeous tenor suggested all the song's sorrow and longing. Richard and I stored the song away, waiting for the moment to use it. (I had been thinking of using the Bundist anthem "Alle Breder" [All Are Brothers], but never found the right place for it.) Once the second act had taken rough shape, Richard found the right moment: the song would underscore the (implied) journey of the brothers from Poland to Canada. Alon recorded it for the production; it played as the brothers watched their homeland disappearing from them.

I later found out why Alon had brought in that particular song. It wasn't simply because it seemed a good match for the story. I heard through the Toronto Jewish grapevine that Alon's grandmother used to sing him that song when he was a boy. Alon hadn't told me this, but after I heard the story a second time, I thought I'd better check it out with Alon before it became a permanent part of his personal history. I asked him about it in an email; he replied:

> "Yam Lid" is a song I sang with the Flying Bulgars [a Toronto-based klezmer band] during my four-month stint as their lead singer.... My bubbie was ailing at the time, but she always got a kick out of correcting my Yiddish. We had a running joke that I was destroying the language. My first performance with the band, with any band ever, was at a huge outdoor venue in El Paso, Texas. El Paso is at the foot of the Rocky Mountain chain and on the border of Mexico; it was hosting a Mariachi festival at the time, so I spent the night before the concert soaking up the brassy charisma of Mexican schmaltz. Huge crowds going wild. The next evening, I walked out on stage, sang Yiddish to 3000 dancing smiling Mex-Texans as the sun set beside the ever-expanding jagged hills. I felt a rush of arrival, of being fully myself and fully connected at the same time. That night, as I was onstage, my bubbie died. I took the first flight home, made it to the funeral and sang "Yam Lid" in her memory. So the story is true in a sense.

II.ix. The most difficult scene to get right. I'm still not sure it *is* right. And it's no coincidence that, like the second most difficult scene to get right (II.ii.), it features the last holdover from *None is Too Many*. This was another instance of letting the historical facts get in the way of a good story. It was also proof positive that you can't lift material from one play—even your own—and plunk it down in another. There were other scenes I tried to parachute in from *None is Too Many*, but in the end not one word of the earlier play made it into this one.

II.x. In contrast to Blair, I found myself writing King with great confidence. I once heard Edward Albee—speaking to a roomful of young playwrights—say that you shouldn't start to write until you know your characters well enough to imagine what they might say on any subject, in any circumstance. I imagine my characters on paper. Oh, I do plenty of mulling, but a scene in your head is only as good as its realisation on paper, and then again only as good as its representation on stage. But it says here that you gotta start somewhere, and for me that somewhere is in front of a blank screen, staring down a blinking cursor. Some writers start with outlines. (If you work in TV or film, you have no choice but to start with an outline.) I don't get it. How can you know the scene until you know the characters? And how can you know

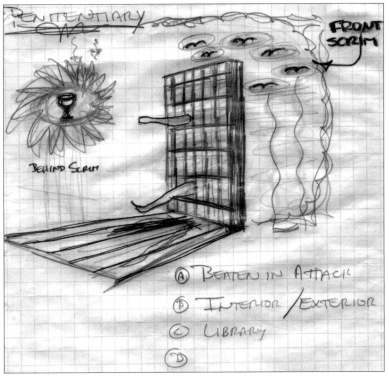

Original lighting design sketch
by Graeme Thomson.

the characters until you know how they speak and think and act? Knowing what a character might say or do doesn't mean that he'll never surprise you; it means he's alive in your imagination. I knew, for example, that King would have to accede to Joseph's dissembling attempt to secure his family's visas, but as to what he would say, how he would react along the way to giving consent, these things didn't exist on some chart. After the first read-through of the scene, which went without a hitch (no fumbling with the words), there was a brief silence in the room. The actors kept staring at the pages in their hands. Finally, mercifully, someone said, "Great scene." But then it had been read during week two of the rehearsal period, and had the added bonus of being a freshly minted scene. The question was whether it would hold up to close scrutiny. It did. I made one small cut during previews, but otherwise, this was a case of getting it right the first time – and not making changes for the sake of change.

II.xi. The scene nearly got away from me. I lost confidence in an early version of it, started to second-guess it, over-think it. One afternoon I came in with a new draft that I figured would knock people out. It did anything but. The actors were sitting pell-mell in the rehearsal room during the read-through, which seemed dull, uninspired. True, it was the afternoon, when blood sugar levels are at their lowest; and it was the third week of rehearsal, when the last thing an actor wants to see is a new speech, let along a new scene. But here it was, and the response went from indifference, to puzzlement, to disapproval. Alon expressed the opinion that I had destroyed the simplicity and beauty of the earlier draft of the scene (he used kinder words). I didn't take it well, and fought him on the points he raised. After Richard weighed in, we decided to proceed with the new version, which I argued deserved more than a one-time reading before being shunted aside. The problem is, I knew Alon might have been right. I sought him out on break, and we had a more sober conversation about the scene. I understood his points more clearly, and decided to head back to the keyboard, trying to retain, or at least regain, what had been there in the earlier version, without simply giving in to first draft nostalgia. (Looking at first drafts is like looking at pictures of yourself as a kid; unformed, a little gawky, but so innocent, so fresh, so full of promise.)

The revisions didn't stop. I remember dropping off yet another draft to Richard as he sat at the director's table in the theatre, trying to get through the gruelling technical rehearsals without smoking himself to death. It was very dark, darker than at most tech rehearsals, with very little spill from the stage lights. Richard tried to read the new scene by the light of his table lamp, but there were too many interruptions. (Truth is, I was the interruption.) So outside on break, while I made small talk with the actors, Richard sat a fair distance away and read it. We then went inside, where Richard went through the scene with me, comparing the new draft, line-by-line, to the one they'd been rehearsing with, making sure that he understood each and every beat. I think most directors would have collapsed at this point, or thrown their hands in the air and said "Enough!" or simply barred me from rehearsals and said, "To hell with it. The play isn't perfect, but it's what we have, so let's do the best we can." Well, it's axiomatic that the play isn't perfect, but Richard would never have made such a speech (not with the playwright present, anyway), because he's interested in one thing: making it better. If that means a new speech after the final preview, to be heard for the first time on opening night, so be it. If it means learning the scene all over again—and no matter how close this new version was to the previous one, it was essentially like learning a new scene—then that's what has to happen. I was heading out of town for a couple of days then, off to a bar mitzvah in Ottawa.

Just as well, I think, because it meant that I wouldn't make any more changes. On my return, I discovered that no further changes were necessary, that the revisions were working to everyone's satisfaction. Still, I watched the dress rehearsal nervously, wondering if I'd written the scene to death, hoping that it would hold together. When it did, thanks in no small part to Richard's staging of it, I felt that the changes had been worth it. I found myself caught up in the emotion of the scene, which surprised me, given that we were at the end of the rehearsal period, when everything feels draggy and just plain wrong. But the company was at its finest, and Alex Poch-Goldin (Judah) was especially affecting. Alex is equal parts fire and air, a dangerous, intimidating presence on stage who can also be open, loving and vulnerable. His recognition of Joseph was a moment of poetry.

II.xii. I knew this would be the most difficult scene to write, so when it came time to take another run at the second act, I wrote the last scene first. Maybe I was just in the right mood to write it. Maybe it's a scene I'd been thinking about for five years, since my father died. All I know is that I could only write it using the intense language that I'd used when Jacob was told of the death of Joseph. It was liberating to write at that level, instead of trying to portray the scene as one would in a naturalistic play. On the other hand, there's something very natural about it all, as anyone who's attended the death of a loved one knows. Everything is heightened at that time. You find yourself saying things you didn't know you had it in you to say. You find a kind of eloquence that you're rarely called upon to use. To end the play any other way was unthinkable.

I think it was after the third preview that the theatre was plunged into darkness. An electrical fire that could easily have gotten out of control took out much of the theatre's electricity, including the lobby lights and the circuits for the Mainspace lighting board. We all waited around for word on whether or not the technicians could rig up some lights that would allow us to at least rehearse that day. Rather than sit around in the gloom of the darkened theatre, the bunch of us crowded into the back of a small, drab Chinese restaurant a block away. It was a drizzly, grey day. I had a few script changes to give out, most of which the actors could write by hand into their scripts, but a couple of which required paper to be passed around. So while the waitress took orders and collected menus, I handed out the latest version of the first act synagogue scene. Richard gave acting notes. Then came word that while we could go back to the theatre to rehearse, the preview that night had been cancelled. I think everyone was relieved to hear this. In a way, it seemed right to not have an audience that night. There had been so many changes that we all felt as though we could use another dress rehearsal. And now, with a few divine sparks, we were to have it.

As we stood outside the restaurant, waiting for everyone to emerge, Alon told me about some of the reactions he'd been hearing about the play. People were stunned, he said; in tears. The play meant so much to them. He told me that at the previous night's preview, an elderly man in the audience joined in as the brothers recited kaddish for Jacob.

That night's run-through was the best performance I'd seen; perhaps the best I ever would see. (I usually see every preview, skip the opening, then return about halfway through the run, and again for the final performance.) The actors seemed looser that night, more comfortable. The rehearsal had gone well. The script changes made sense to everyone, and were easily absorbed. The second act, which up to that night had been the weaker sister of the two, now seemed the more mature. Now it was the first act that looked a little ragged and slow. But there were three more previews to fix that imbalance, and no one seemed terribly worried.

I decided that the best thing I could do after that night was to stop writing. It was a signal to the actors that the show was theirs now. Like all good actors, they took the cue.

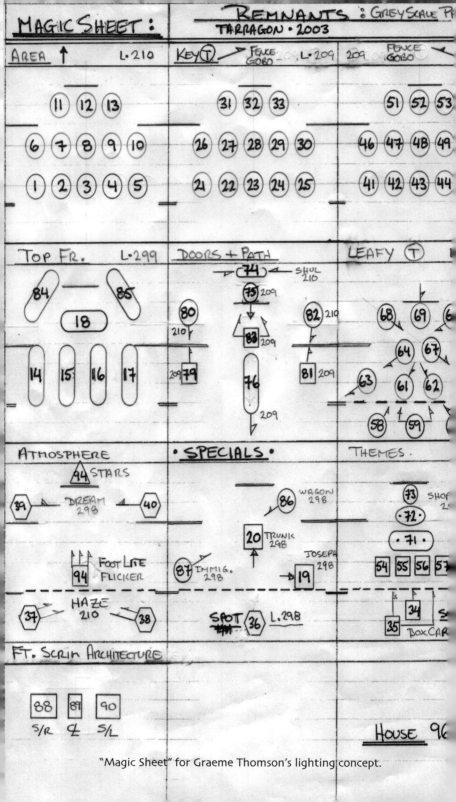

"Magic Sheet" for Graeme Thomson's lighting concept.